Taylor's Pocket Guide to

Perennials for Sun

Taylor's Pocket Guide to

Perennials

for Sun

MAGGIE OSTER
Consulting Editor

A Chanticleer Press Edition
Houghton Mifflin Company
Boston

For information about
permission to reproduce selections from this book,
write to Permissions,
Houghton Mifflin Company, 2 Park Street,
Boston, Massachusetts 02108.

Based on Taylor's Encyclopedia of Gardening, Fourth Edition,
Copyright © 1961 by Norman Taylor,
revised and edited by
Gordon P. DeWolf, Jr.

Prepared and produced by Chanticleer Press, New York
Typeset by Dix Type, Inc., Syracuse, New York
Printed and bound by
Dai Nippon, Tokyo, Japan

Library of Congress Catalog Card Number: 88-46140
ISBN: 0-395-51020-1

00   10   9   8   7   6   5   4   3   2   1

CONTENTS

GARDENING WITH PERENNIALS FOR SUN

PERENNIALS ARE, in many ways, the most rewarding flowers. Once planted, they bloom year after year, repaying you richly for all the time and effort invested in planning and planting your garden. Perennials make low-maintenance flower gardens a reality, yet they offer unlimited opportunities for the gardener who wants to spend time at a hobby.

What is a Perennial?

Plants that bloom for more than one year are called perennials. They may last for a few years or for generations. Technically, trees and shrubs are perennials, but most people when they use the term are denoting the herbaceous perennials, which are the subject of this book. These flowers die back to the ground in winter, but their roots remain alive throughout the winter. It is through these persistent rootstocks that the plants renew themselves the following growing season.

First Steps Toward Planting

No other plants are as versatile and offer so much variety to the gardener as perennials. No matter where you garden, in the country or the city, on a small terrace or an acre of land, in sun or in shade, a great many perennials will grow and flourish there. The key to success is to choose the right plants for your environment.

The perennials in this book are easy to find and easy to care for. All grow well in full sun; many will also tolerate some degree of shade. By and large, they can be grown in many environments around the North American continent.

The perennials that you select must be able to grow in your garden. Some perennials are so hardy that they can survive almost anywhere; others can only live within certain temperature or humidity ranges.

Plant hardiness is based on three factors: temperature, availability of water, and soil conditions. Of these, temperature is by far the most important. The U.S. Department of Agriculture has devised a map that divides North America into ten zones based on minimum winter temperature. (See pages 106–107.) Zone 1 is the coldest, with winter lows of $-50°$ F; zone 10 is the warmest, with winter minimums of $30°$ to $40°$ F, and is often frost-free. Knowing the zone in which you live is particularly useful when you buy a plant you have never grown before. If the description in this book says "zone 4," it means that the perennial is hardy to zone 4, but will not generally survive winters colder than zone 4.

Microclimates

Within each zone, conditions can fluctuate because of variations in temperature, rainfall, or soil type. These microclimates can occur within states, cities, or even on a small plot of land.

For example, the temperature may be colder on the north side of your house than it is elsewhere. Similarly, colder-than-normal temperatures often occur at the bottom of hills or on ground that is exposed to wind. Areas that receive plenty of sun are usually warmer than those that do not, as are areas that are protected from the wind and those that receive reflected heat in the winter.

Successful gardening is based, in part, on understanding how these variations affect your garden. By learning to recognize the microclimates on your land, you will be able to grow a wider variety of plants than if you based all your plant choices on zone.

Sun and Shade

When you are determining how much sun a plant requires, keep latitude in mind. In the Deep South, midsummer days are relatively short and the nights are long. In the far North, midsummer days are very long. This extra light can make plants grow rapidly in the North, while those in the South may grow more slowly.

Even when perennials are said to require full sun, they usually don't need sun for the entire day. In the heat of summer, most plants benefit from some shade to protect them from intense sunlight. In the South, this protection is especially important. If a plant has morning sun, and then receives some shade from the shadow of a building, fence, hedge, or tree in the afternoon, it will flourish. Sun-loving plants will often thrive if they receive shade during the most intense heat of the day, and then have late-afternoon sun. They will also survive if they get filtered light throughout the day.

Buying Perennial Plants

A perennial garden gives you the chance to explore a delightful range of color, shape, and form. Some gardeners start plants from seeds, cuttings, or divisions donated by friends and neighbors. Most perennials, however, come either from local garden centers and specialty nurseries or by mail order. You'll probably find yourself acquiring plants from a variety of sources, because each has its advantages.

When you buy plants locally, you can see what you are getting and choose the plants individually. Plants are likely to be larger than those bought through the mail, and they will make an instant show in the garden. Since plants in garden centers are usually sold in pots, they may be held in a shady spot until it suits your schedule to plant them. Examine plants carefully to be sure they are healthy.

Mail-order sources frequently offer a wider selection of plants than do garden centers. Mail-order companies often ship bare-root plants, and these demand immediate attention upon their arrival.

Price alone is not a reliable criterion for choosing one plant source over another, since cost is not always an indication of plant size or quality. If possible, try to get recommendations from another gardener, or place a small order at first with a company you've never tried before.

Getting Started

Most perennials prefer soils that are loamy, well drained, and high in organic matter. Many plants that do well in poor soil will grow even better in richer soil. Organic matter may be peat moss, humus, rotted leaves or plants, or composted material; it acts like a sponge to help the soil retain water and nutrients, yet allows adequate air to pass to the roots of the plants. Organic matter also activates organisms in the soil that break down soil particles and fertilizers to release plant nutrients.

A soil's pH level measures its level of acidity or alkalinity, factors that influence the uptake of secondary and micronutrients. pH is rated on a scale from 1–14, with 7 representing a neutral level. The lower numbers indicate acidity, the higher ones alkalinity.

Although perennials are not overly fussy, most prefer a slightly acid to neutral soil (with a pH of 5.5–7.5). Adding lime to the soil will make it more alkaline, and sulfur or peat moss will make it more acid. To determine the pH level of your soil, either buy a simple soil test kit or send a soil sample to a local soil test lab.

Fertilizer

A complete fertilizer contains nitrogen, phosphorus, and potassium. The percentage of each of these elements in the mixture is described by three numbers on the package, such as 5–10–5, 10–10–10, 10–6–4, or some other formula.

Most perennials grown for their flowers do best with a fertilizer that is relatively low in nitrogen, because too much nitrogen encourages the growth of foliage at the cost of flowers. Fertilizer can be applied in a granular form when the bed is prepared, as a liquid after planting, or in time-release pellets.

Preparing the Soil

Because perennials live for many years in the same spot, it is worth the effort to prepare the soil well before you plant them. Doing so allows plants to establish good root systems. Even if you choose to move the plants, well-prepared soil will make it easier to lift and divide them.

Before working the soil, determine how wet it is. Take a handful and squeeze it tightly. If it contains too much moisture, the soil will compact and become unfit for growing. If you find the soil too wet to work, wait for three or four days, then test it again.

To prepare a new bed, first turn the soil over to a depth of one spade (about 18–20 inches). Next, spread a layer of compost, peat moss, or other organic material over the soil surface. The amount of granular fertilizer you add depends upon soil test results; an average amount is five pounds of 5–10–10 per 100 square feet. If your soil is very acid you may want to add lime, again following the recommendations on the package. Since most soils in the United States are low in phosphorus, gardeners customarily add five pounds of superphosphate (0–46–0) per 100 square feet of bed. Mix the phosphorus in thoroughly, since it tends to stay where it is placed.

Incorporate the organic material, fertilizer, lime, and phosphorus into the soil by turning them in with a spade or by rototilling. Finally, rake the ground smooth.

Planting the Perennials

The perfect planting day is cool, cloudy, and calm; otherwise choose late afternoon. If you are planting a new bed, lay the plants in their pots out on the ground according to your design and move them around until you are satisfied with the arrangement. If the bed is too deep to reach across without stepping into the freshly prepared soil, place a wide board across the bed and use it as a bridge. Using a hand trowel, dig a hole for each plant, remove it from its pot, and set it in the hole. If your plant came potted in a soilless medium of peat and vermiculite, combine part of the mix with garden soil to ease root transition from the lighter medium to the heavier one. Firm the soil around the plant using your fingers.

If mail-order plants appear dried out when they arrive, soak them in a one-quarter strength water-soluble fertilizer solution for an hour before planting or potting up.

When working with an existing bed, set the plants out in the bed on top of the ground. Once you are satisfied with the position, mark the location, remove the plants, and dig the holes. Add organic matter and other amendments to the soil removed from the hole and incorporate your additions thoroughly. Plant as directed above.

Once the plants are in the ground, water them well. Be sure the plants are soaked thoroughly and deeply. If the weather is hot or especially dry, water the plants every three or four days until they are established and new growth begins, unless an inch of rain falls in a week.

Maintaining the Perennial Bed

Even the simplest of low-maintenance gardens requires some upkeep. Although some tasks may, in the abstract, seem like work, you will find that your enjoyment of your garden increases in direct proportion to the amount of care you put in.

Weeding

No gardener can avoid weeding, but you can make the job less time-consuming if you catch weeds when they are young. Weeds will become worse each year if you do not keep on top of removing them. Adding a layer of mulch to the perennial bed also keeps invasive growth in check. Where weeds are a serious problem, spread a sheet of black plastic (available at garden centers) on the soil, punching holes in it so water can pass through, and cover it with an organic mulch of wood chips to camouflage it. If you keep your beds free of weeds, you will be able to remove the plastic in two years.

Fertilizing

Although you added fertilizer at planting time, an application of fertilizer each year afterwards will be necessary. For perennials, use a fertilizer whose second number on the label is equal to or higher than the first number. Spread the fertilizer on the ground in spring when growth starts or when the plants are in bud. Plants that require heavy fertilizing should be fed when growth starts, in early summer, and eight weeks before the first fall frost. Apply fertilizer to moist soil and water it well after application.

Water

In the heat of summer, and through periods of drought, water your plants regularly. Soak them deeply, and avoid getting the foliage wet if possible. If you use a sprinkler or nozzled hose to water from overhead, do so in the morning. Light waterings, even if frequent, do more harm than good by discouraging deep roots. New plants may require daily watering, especially if it is hot, dry or windy.

Mulching

A mulch is a protective covering that is spread over the soil and around the bases of plants; mulches conserve soil moisture, suppress weeds, and keep the root zone cooler than the air temperature. Mulching also saves work by reducing the need for manual weeding. Apply the mulch thickly, as it will eventually mat down, and avoid placing it too close to plant crowns, where it may encourage diseases and slugs.

When you choose a mulch, consider its availability, cost, appearance, and durability. Organic materials, such as bark chips, leaves, hay, pine boughs, and compost, benefit the soil and are generally preferable to man-made mulching materials. Some mulches will increase the acidity of the soil; others, such as wood chips, may blow around in windy areas and prove a nuisance. Some mulches are potential fire hazards; others may contain weed seeds or diseases that could be transmitted to your plants. If in doubt, describe your situation to your local nursery professionals and ask their advice.

Staking

Some perennials produce many stems that tend to flop over if they are not staked. Others are very tall and need support to keep them upright and protected from wind. You can use bamboo sticks, wooden poles, or wire devices similar to tomato cages. When you insert the stake into the ground, be careful not to damage the plant's crown or roots. When tying plants to a stake, use natural twine or twist-ties, and tie loosely so as not to damage the stem.

Pinching and Disbudding

The removal of a small amount of a plant's growing tip to encourage branching or to modify flowering is known as pinching. Pinching plants once or twice in the spring, usually before the first of July, will cause plants to be shorter, sturdier, and produce more but smaller flowers.

With perennials such as delphinium, some gardeners prefer several large stems of flowers to many smaller stems. In spring, pinch out all but one or two stems per plant.

Disbudding is another method of changing the style of flowers produced. Removal of side buds encourages the main bud to produce larger, showier blooms. You can also remove the central bud instead of the side buds to produce a more even spray of smaller flowers.

Throughout the gardening season, remove faded flowers and flowering stalks to improve the plant's appearance and conserve the energy. Cleaning up like this extends the growing season and, in some cases, induces a second bloom.

Fall Cleanup

In the autumn, before the first killing frost, clean flower beds of all dead foliage to reduce disease and eliminate areas where insects can overwinter. Don't cut back ornamental grasses, though, until spring; they will be beautiful for most of the winter. After the ground has frozen, protect newly planted and marginally hardy plants with a layer of pine boughs over the plants, covered with leaves. Once the weather begins to warm in the spring, remove the covering.

Cold Frames

If you are going to grow plants from seed or from cuttings, a cold frame is a useful and versatile device. It is basically a bottomless box with a transparent top of glass, Plexiglas, or Fiberglas, which can be opened or removed. Cold frames can be homemade or purchased as prefabricated units. They are best placed against a south-facing wall, hedge, or fence. The soil inside should be well drained and rich in organic matter.

Seeds

Raising perennials from seed for one's own garden is simple, but it often takes a long time before plants reach blooming size. Outdoors you can sow seeds directly into the bed or the cold frame; inside you can start them in pots or flats, then transport them to the frame or garden when the weather becomes warm. When starting from seeds, always follow the directions on the seed packet.

If you start seeds indoors, use a sterile seed-starting mixture. Once germinated, plants need the bright light of a greenhouse or sunny window; seedlings may also be grown under fluorescent lights. Tender seedlings must be acclimatized, or "hardened off," before they are set outside. To harden off seedlings, place them in a sheltered, lightly shaded location outdoors for several days, then move to a sheltered sunny spot for several more before planting. Beware of cold night temperatures; bring them back indoors if cold is expected.

Divisions

Dividing perennials not only increases the number of plants, but also rejuvenates older plants that may show signs of straggling or loss of bloom. Although herbaceous perennials vary in their root formation, the majority spread by the development of growth buds, or eyes. Each bud, although attached to the parent plant, grows independently. Propagation by division involves the separation of these growth buds to increase the number of plants. Most perennials can be divided; it is usually the simplest and quickest method of propagation for the gardener.

Plants like peonies and daylilies have fleshy rootstocks. When you dig them out, you'll notice that the roots intertwine and that there are several growth buds on each root. Pull these roots apart gently or cut them with a knife to get several independent pieces, each with one or more growth buds. Plant the pieces in a prepared bed.

In tuberous-rooted plants such as irises, the stem branches out at or below the soil surface. At each underground node on the stem, you will find a bud and one or more roots. If the clump is large, pull the stems apart, making sure that each stem has one or more growth buds. If the clump has only one stem, cut the individual growth buds apart, making sure that each bud has one or more roots.

Perennials such as Coral Bells and *Ajuga* develop many crowns. Dig up the plant and carefully pull the crowns apart. Plants such as False Dragonhead and asters, which have numerous stems (each with growth buds), can also be dug up and pulled or cut apart.

In colder areas, it is better to divide plants in the spring before the foliage is two inches high. In milder climates, divide the perennials in early fall after they have finished blooming. If you are dealing with plants that are very overgrown, first cut the plant back to the ground and lift the entire clump. To separate a large clump, insert two digging forks back to back into the center and push them apart. You can also cut the plant apart with a sharp spade or an ax, or pull small clumps apart with your fingers.

After the plants are divided, treat any cut surfaces with a fungicide. Replant the divisions, taking care to place the crowns at the proper depth, and then water them. Give plants divided in the fall adequate winter protection.

Cuttings

Another method of propagating perennials is by either stem or root cuttings. Plants such as chrysanthemums, asters, false sunflowers, and some others are easy to increase by stem cuttings. Take the cuttings in late spring or early summer, using side shoots or the less vigorous longer shoots. There should be a minimum of three leaf joints. With a razor blade or sharp knife, cut the shoot one-quarter to one-half inch below a leaf or pair of leaves. The new roots will come out below the node where the stem buds are located in the axils of the leaves.

Immediately place the cuttings in a pot or flat of moistened, sterile, soilless potting mix. Space the cuttings so the leaves barely touch. Remove the lowest leaves of the cuttings and push the stem gently down. After you have inserted all the cuttings, cover the pot or flat with plastic film, using a wire frame or wooden stakes to keep the bag from touching the cuttings. Place the container in indirect light, never in sunlight. Watch for signs of discoloration or disease, and remove any plants with these symptoms. After the plants are rooted, remove the bag. You will know that roots have formed when you see new growth and when the cuttings resist a gentle tug.

Poppies, anemones, and phlox can be propagated from root cuttings. Dig up the roots in midsummer or in the fall after they have lost their foliage. Cut the roots in one- to two-inch pieces. Place the cuttings into a container of moist sand and put in a cool area. Keep moist but not wet. Transplant rooted cuttings into separate pots, then plant outdoors when all danger of frost is past.

Garden Design

Any garden is the product of its owner, its designer, and the person who maintains it. In real life, most of us play all of these roles at once. A good design must therefore be suited to the site selected by the owner as well as to the time and energy of the person who maintains it.

Whether you start with a new plot of land or a preexisting garden, the first step is to draw a base map. This is a simple sketch that tells you what is on the property, including existing buildings, fences, drives, and so forth.

On a photocopy of your base map, note microclimates or other factors that will influence plant growth. Mark any rock outcroppings, high areas, low areas, or spots with poor drainage. Indicate windy sites, poor views, and areas with shade. Now you can begin to plan where to plant perennials.

Site Selection

The traditional way to grow perennials is in a formal border or flower garden where there is a backdrop such as a wall, hedge, or shrub planting. In such a design, the plants are arranged with the tallest in the back and the shortest in the front. Perennials may also be used in island beds, set into the lawn, although these require extra maintenance since the grass must be cut and trimmed on all sides. In these beds, the taller plants are placed in the center and all plants are graded from the tall center to the low edges.

Perennials may also be grouped by specialty use or to suit a specific site. You can have alpine plants in a rock garden, bog plants in a wet area, meadow flowers in a field, or a groundcover planting under trees or on slopes where grass does not grow or is too difficult to cut.

You can also grow perennials in containers or planters, but you may have a problem with winter hardiness. In containers, all but the hardiest of perennials will require some form of protection against the winter or need replanting on an annual basis. Insulating the container or moving it to an unheated area out of the wind is usually sufficient. Containers must have adequate drainage and should be large enough to prevent the plants from blowing over in the wind and drying out. Garden containers work well on terraces or balconies, or other similar areas.

Choosing Plants

When selecting perennials, consider the color, height, spread, time of bloom, and special growing requirements of each plant. With careful selection, you can have flowers in bloom throughout the growing season.

Color

The choice of color combinations is essentially a personal one, but there are some basic facts that can help you decide what colors to use in the garden. Perennials which bloom at different times throughout the growing season, allow you to vary the color scheme. It can be yellow and red in the spring fading to blue, pink, and white in the summer and ending with deep reds, bronzes, and yellow-golds in the fall.

Colors are grouped in two basic categories, the warm colors and the cool colors. Warm colors are reds, oranges, and yellows. They are also known as advancing colors because they draw the eye and make the object seem closer than it really is. The cool colors are blue, violet, and green. They are known as receding colors because they make the objects appear farther away. Careful use of these groups can make a small space seem larger or a larger space closer.

Colors that offer great contrast, such as red and green or blue and orange, can add drama to a garden. Colors that are closely related, such as blue and violet or red and orange, are more harmonious. Pastels tend to be more subtle, and white can offset harsh contrasts. If you plan to use large masses of brilliant colors and you do not want a lot of drama, separate the colors with green foliage, silvery foliage, or white flowers. These will soften the dramatic effect. Sun and shadow also affect color. Shadow darkens tones; sun intensifies them.

Once you have completed your base map, listed the plants of your choice, and decided on the colors you like, it can all be put together. Make sure you have a good mix of flower shapes and foliage. In the perennial garden, foliage offers interest and acts as a background for the flowers. Since foliage usually lasts longer than the flowers, you will want to give this feature of your design careful consideration. Place the names of the selected plants on the base map in their appropriate location. Based on the number of square feet designated for that plant, and the recommended spacing, calculate how many plants you need and place your orders.

A Note on Plant Names

The common, or English, names of plants are often colorful and evocative, but they vary widely from region to region.

Sometimes two different plants have the same or similar common name; some plants have no English name at all. Fortunately, every plant is assigned a scientific (or Latin) name that is distinct and unique to that plant. Scientific names are not necessarily "better," but they are standard around the world and governed by an international set of rules. Therefore, even though scientific names may at first seem difficult or intimidating, they are in the long run a simple and sure way of getting a handle on the plant you want.

A scientific name has two parts. The first is called the generic name: it tells us to which genus (plural, genera) a plant belongs. The second part of the name tells us the species. (A species is a kind of plant or animal that is capable of reproducing with members of its kind, but genetically isolated from others. *Homo sapiens* is a species.) Most genera have several to many species: *Chrysanthemum,* for example, has more than 100. *Chrysanthemum coccineum* is a species included in this book. Scientific names are always italicized or underlined; usually, the generic name is capitalized and the species name is not, but there are exceptions.

The names of naturally occurring varieties are also in italics; they form a third part of the scientific name. The names of cultivars (cultivated varieties, developed by plant breeders) are usually in roman type, enclosed by single quotation marks. They may follow a one- or two-part scientific name, as in *Campanula carpatica* 'Isobel'. Although cultivars and varieties are technically different, they may be treated by the gardener in the same way.

A hybrid is a plant that is the result of a cross between two genera, two species, or two varieties or cultivars. Sometimes hybrids are given a new scientific name, but they are usually indicated by an × within the scientific name. *Aster × frikartii* is a hybrid included in this book.

Organization of the Plant Descriptions

The plant accounts in this book are arranged alphabetically by scientific name. If you know only the common name of a flower, look the plant up in the index under its common name and refer to the page listed.

Some accounts in the book deal with a garden plant at the level of genus, because the genus includes many similar species that are treated in more or less the same way in the garden. In these accounts, only the genus name is given at the top of the page; the name of the species, cultivar, or hybrid pictured is noted within the text.

A Reward of Enduring Beauty

Now you have at your fingertips all the basic information you will need to plant, grow, and maintain beautiful perennials. A little energy, coupled with natural enthusiasm, will bring you a reward of enduring beauty. So, turn now to the individual plant accounts and begin to dream about the color that can be yours in a garden of sun-loving perennials.

Perennials for Sun

Fernleaf Yarrow (*Achillea filipendulina*)

Drought resistant and relatively free of pests, the Fernleaf Yarrows are a staple of the low-maintenance garden. The aromatic foliage is topped with flat flower heads up to 5 inches across. Blooming from early summer to midsummer, these flowers may be used in fresh or dried arrangements. A number of cultivars exist, including 'Gold Plate' (seen here), 4½ feet tall with yellow flowers, and 'Coronation Gold', growing to 3 feet tall with mustard-yellow, 4-inch blooms. This latter variety is vigorous and tolerates heat well but requires staking.

GROWING TIPS

Fernleaf Yarrow needs well-drained soil that is not particularly rich. Plant in groups of 3 or singly, 10–12 inches apart. Remove faded flowers to encourage fall blooming. To retain the best yellow color when dried, cut flowers before the pollen forms. Divide plants about every 4 years in early spring to keep them vigorous.

Common Yarrow *(Achillea millefolium)*

Also called Milfoil, this yarrow grows to 24 inches tall. It tends to spread more than other types, but unless the soil is rich, it will not be invasive. The flat-topped flower clusters of the variety 'Fire King', seen here, are 2–3 inches across; they are produced over a 4–5-week period in midsummer. The leaves are bright green and finely dissected. Other varieties include 'Red Beauty', with crimson flowers; 'Roseum', with rose-pink flowers, and 'White Beauty' with pure white flowers.

GROWING TIPS

Common Yarrow needs moist but well-drained soil of average fertility. For the most landscape impact, plant in groups of 3 about 12 inches apart. Remove faded flowers to encourage fall blooming. Divide plants about every 4 years to rejuvenate them.

Pearly Everlasting *(Anaphalis triplinervis)*

Aperennial native to the Himalayas, Pearly Everlasting is an excellent, if subtle, addition to the garden. It will grow on moist sites, where other gray-foliaged plants will not survive, but will not tolerate drought. The loose clusters of ½-inch flowers bloom throughout midsummer. They are easily dried for winter bouquets and craft projects. Cut the flowers when the center shows, put in a vase with water for several hours, then hang upside down to dry. Plants grow in clumps 12–18 inches tall; 'Summer Snow' is a shorter-growing cultivar useful as an edging.

GROWING TIPS

Pearly Everlasting needs moist, well-drained soil of average fertility. Plant in groups of 3, about 10 inches apart. Divide about every 4 years in the spring or fall.

Japanese Anemone *(Anemone vitifolia)*

The best of the anemones for the garden, Japanese Anemones complement the other flowers of autumn. They look and grow well in front of shrubs or a wall facing south; this also protects them from northern winds. The blooms, 2–3 inches across, appear from late summer until frost on 2- to 3-foot stems; their height makes them good for cutting. Japanese Anemones have dark green, leathery, deeply lobed leaves. 'Robustissima' is pictured. Other varieties are available, but they are less hardy and not as easy to grow.

GROWING TIPS

Japanese Anemones need rich, moist soil that is well drained in winter; 'Robustissima' is the most tolerant of drought and withstands hot summers and sun well. These flowers spread rapidly and should be given plenty of room; plant in groups of 3, 18 inches apart. With slight protection in the fall, plants will continue blooming even after frost. Mulch lightly with oak leaves or pine boughs in the winter in northern areas, after the ground is thoroughly frozen. Plants should not be moved unless necessary.

Golden Marguerite *(Anthemis tinctoria)*

Over a long flowering season in summer, Golden Marguerite bears daisylike flowers, excellent for cutting and nearly 2 inches wide. The bushy clumps of aromatic, finely cut gray-green foliage grow 2–3 feet high; in warmer climates it is evergreen. There are several popular hybrids, including golden-orange 'Beauty of Grallagh', golden-yellow 'Kelwayi', pale yellow 'Moonlight' (pictured), and 'Pale Moon', which changes from light canary yellow to ivory white. Also called Yellow Camomile.

Growing Tips

Space plants 12–16 inches apart. Golden Marguerite tolerates hot, dry climates, but in areas with extremely long, hot summers a little extra moisture, humus, and shade is beneficial. Plants often need to be divided either every year or every other year, as they become bare in the middle. Remove faded flowers to extend the flowering period and prevent unwanted seedlings.

Common Columbine *(Aquilegia canadensis)*

Native to the woodlands of the eastern United States, the Common Columbine grows along rock ledges and readily self-sows in the wild. The unusual late-spring-blooming flowers are 1½ inches wide, with yellow petals and red sepals and spurs. The Common Columbine is excellent for a rock garden or flower border. It grows 1–2 feet tall with compound, blue-green leaves. There are other species as well as many colorful hybrids in shades of red, yellow, blue, white, pink, or purple and varying in height from 3 inches to 3 feet.

GROWING TIPS

Columbines do best in open, sandy loam with excellent drainage; however, overly dry soil is not tolerated. Plant in full sun to partial shade, 12 inches apart. If you don't want the plants to self-sow, remove the faded flowers and seed pods. Leafminers may mar foliage, but the health of the plants is not affected; to control, remove and destroy damaged plant parts. Plants may be divided in the early spring or fall.

Wall Cress *(Arabis caucasica)*

Masses of fragrant, ½-inch white flowers in early spring cover these ground-hugging, cascading plants. Excellent for cutting, the flowers practically obscure the gray-green leaves. Grow Wall Cress in the rock garden or at the front of a flower border. The variety 'Snow Cap' is pictured. There is a double-flowered form, 'Flore Pleno', as well as a variety with pink flowers, ('Coccineum') and one with variegated foliage ('Variegata'). Rock Cress, *Arabis procurrens,* forms a thick mat of shining, evergreen leaves with tiny white flowers in spring.

GROWING TIPS

Wall Cress must have good drainage and grows well in average to sandy soil. Space plants 8–12 inches apart in full sun. Although Wall Cress thrives in sun and heat, it tends to rot in areas with high humidity. Cut the plants back after flowering to encourage branching and better-shaped plants. Plants can be divided in spring or fall.

Silver Mound Artemisia
(Artemisia schmidtiana) Zone 4

The neatly sculpted clumps of Silver Mound Artemisia grow about 6 inches tall, with a spread of 12–18 inches. The tiny, pale flowers are insignificant, but the bright, silvery foliage is soft and silken. Several plants added to the front of the flower border provide a striking accent, particularly to red, pink, yellow, or blue flowers. Other artemisias are valued for their aromatic, ornamental gray or silver leaves. Silver King Artemisia *(A. ludoviciana* var. *albula),* with thin gray-green leaves, grows 3 feet tall; it is hardy to zone 5. Lambrook Silver Wormwood *(A. absinthium* 'Lambrook Silver') has fine-textured, silky leaves on plants 3 feet tall.

Growing Tips
Artemisias need very well-drained soils, doing better in poor and sandy ones than in rich ones. Space plants 12 inches apart in full sun. Prune the foliage before flowering to prevent clumps from opening in the middle. Artemisias are easily increased by root division.

Butterfly Weed (*Asclepias tuberosa*)

If Butterfly Weed were not a native meadow flower, it would perhaps be more widely grown, for it is a most undemanding, spectacular flower for the low-maintenance garden. Long-lasting when cut, Butterfly Weed blooms in midsummer, producing 2-inch or larger clusters of ½-inch flowers. All sorts of butterflies as well as other insects in search of sweet nectar are attracted to the flowers. Forms with red or yellow flowers are available as well as the orange. The flowers are followed by the seed pods and winged seeds typical of its relative, the milkweed. These long-lived plants grow 1–3 feet tall. Also called Pleurisy-Root, for its medicinal use by native Americans.

GROWING TIPS

Butterfly Weed needs well-drained, average to sandy soil. Set plants 10–16 inches apart in full sun. Provide water during periods of prolonged drought. To increase, divide plants in spring, being sure to dig deeply to get all of the roots, or start plants from seed.

Aster Hybrids *(Aster × frikartii)*

A group of hybrid varieties that are considered among the best for any garden, these asters grow 2–3 feet tall and produce lavender-blue flowers from midsummer into fall. Each fragrant gold-centered flower is 2–3 inches across. The variety 'Monch' has richly colored flowers and rather upright growth. The flowers of 'Wonder of Staffa' are slightly more lavender and the growth a bit sprawling.

GROWING TIPS

Aster × frikartii must have well-drained, fertile, moist soil. During the growing season, the soil must not become dry; during the dormant season, it must not become soggy. Set plants 12–24 inches apart in full sun. Remove faded flowers to prolong the blooming season. To lessen sprawling, pinch plants back once in early summer. Mildew may be a problem in humid areas; spray with sulfur or benomyl. North of zone 7, mulch with pine boughs in winter. Transplant young plants from the outside of the clump in the spring.

New England Aster *(Aster novae-angliae)*   Zone 5

A staple of the flower border because of the late summer and fall bloom, the New England Aster is one of our native plants that has risen to deserving popularity. Dozens of varieties are available, ranging in colors from white to varying shades of pink, red, lavender, blue, and purple. Height ranges from 3–5 feet; the flower heads are usually 1½ inches across.

GROWING TIPS

New England Asters need soil that is fertile, moist, and well drained. During the growing season the soil must remain moist, but during the dormant season, it must never be soggy. Space plants 12–24 inches apart in full sun. Staking may be necessary with taller types to prevent them sprawling and falling over. Remove faded flowers to keep asters from self-sowing. Fungus diseases may be a problem in humid areas. Plants need division every other year; divisions from the outside of the clumps grow quickly.

Basket-of-Gold *(Aurinia saxitilis)*

This perennial is the most popular of the madworts, a group of herbs belonging to the mustard family. Plants grow to 6–12 inches high, forming dense mats or clumps. The golden-yellow flowers, ⅛ inch across, appear in spring in clusters that cover the grayish foliage. Two popular cultivars are 'Compacta', known for its dwarf habit, and 'Citrina', pictured, with pale yellow flowers.

GROWING TIPS

The madworts are easy to grow in dry, well-drained soil with a sunny exposure. They need excellent drainage; hot, humid conditions can prove fatal. Soil that is too fertile will cause plants to sprawl. To lengthen the life span of this plant, cut stems back by one-half to one-third after flowering.

Blue False Indigo *(Baptisia australis)*

Native to eastern parts of North America, Blue False Indigo is an indispensable perennial for those who can't seem to grow anything else. Use it in the middle to the rear of the low-maintenance perennial border or as an accent plant. In late spring, plants 3–5 feet tall bear 9- to 12-inch spikes of dark blue, pealike flowers, each 1 inch across. After these fade, attractive black seed pods develop that can be used in dried arrangements. The dark blue-green, 3-part oval leaves stay in good condition throughout the growing season.

GROWING TIPS
Plant Blue False Indigo in open, porous, sandy soil. Space plants 18–24 inches apart in full sun. Blue False Indigo tolerates a wide range of soils; it lives for many years in one spot, seldom needs dividing, is not bothered by insects or diseases, is not invasive, and does not need staking. Propagated from seeds or by division, plants may be slow to grow for the first season or so after transplanting.

Blackberry Lily *(Belamcanda chinensis)*

This exotic-looking relative of the iris bears 2-inch speckled flowers on 3- to 4-foot stems thoughout July and August. The faded flowers twist curiously before dropping off. Later, seed pods burst open to reveal shiny black clusters of seeds resembling a blackberry; these last a long time and are attractive in dried arrangements. The leaves of Blackberry Lily are sword shaped, much like those of an iris, and grow 2 to 4 feet tall. A shorter species, *B. flabellata,* grows 10–12 inches tall; the cultivar 'Hello Yellow' has unspotted yellow flowers.

GROWING TIPS

Blackberry Lily grows best in moist, fertile soil that is not soggy in winter, but it tolerates a wide range of well-drained soils. Space plants 10–14 inches apart in sun to partial shade, using 1 or 2 plants near the front or middle of the flower border. Plants readily self-sow, but the seedlings are easily removed if not desired. Although dividing is seldom necessary, plants may also be propagated by division of the stout rootstock in spring.

Boltonia *(Boltonia asteroides)*

In late summer and early fall, Boltonia bears asterlike flowers, distinguished by the long, smooth, toothless, gray-green leaves. Sometimes called False Camomile, False Starwort, or Thousand-Flowered Aster, Boltonia forms 3- to 5-foot-tall bushy plants suitable for the back of the flower border. Although the flowers are only ¾ inch across, they are very numerous and showy. The white cultivar 'Snowbank' is pictured; there are also lilac and violet-purple forms. Native to eastern North America, Boltonia is an excellent complement in the garden to New England Aster and Golden Aster *(Chrysopsis)*.

GROWING TIPS

Boltonias are very easy to grow in average soil, but will grow fastest in moist, fertile soil. Space plants 18 inches apart in full sun. Plants are easily propagated by spring or fall division; this is usually required at least every other year to keep plants healthy and attractive. Some varieties need staking.

Finger Poppy Mallow *(Callirhoe involucrata)* Zone 4

The long, trailing stems of Finger Poppy Mallow bear flowers in various shades from reddish purple to rose-crimson, cherry red, and rose with white centers. Blooming throughout summer into early fall, the flowers are 1½–2½ inches across. Poppy Mallow has hardy, 5- or 7-lobed leaves on plants that grow 6–12 inches. Excellent for the front of the border, the rock garden, or trailing over a bank or stone wall, Finger Poppy Mallow is also a good choice for a seaside garden.

GROWING TIPS

Poppy Mallow is easy to grow in ordinary garden soil with excellent drainage. Because of its deep tap root, it needs water only during droughts. Space 10–20 inches apart in full sun. Plants need propagation at least every other year in the spring or fall from seeds or cuttings. Plants propagated by division in the spring or fall may be slow to become established.

Carpathian Harebell (*Campanula carpatica*) Zone 4

The most popular of the small-growing campanulas, the Carpathian Harebell is excellent for the front of the flower border, as an edging, or in a rock garden. Growing 6–12 inches tall, this native of southern Europe has toothed, oval leaves 1½ inches long. Plants grow in dense clumps, about 8 inches across. The upward-facing, cuplike flowers are 2 inches wide and are borne individually on wiry stems from late spring to midsummer. Pictured is the variety 'Isobel'; others include 'Blue Clips', with sky-blue flowers, 'Wedgewood Blue', with flat, violet-blue flowers, and 'White Clips', with white blooms.

GROWING TIPS

Carpathian Harebells are easy to grow in cool, moist, fertile, well-drained soil that is neutral to slightly acid. Space plants 12 inches apart in sun to partial shade. Plants will bloom over a longer period if faded flowers are removed. A winter mulch of pine boughs, straw, or hay is advised in the colder limits of the hardiness range.

Adriatic Bellflower *(Campanula garganica)*

The sprawling, 6-inch stems of Adriatic Bellflower are covered with flat clusters of star-shaped, ½-inch flowers in spring. Blooms continue to be produced sporadically until fall. This creeping trailer is useful in the rock garden, at the front of the flower border, or along a wall. The Dalmatian Bellflower *(C. portenschlagiana)* is a similar species. It grows 6–8 inches tall, with bluish-purple, 1-inch flowers from late spring to summer; it is hardy to zone 5.

GROWING TIPS

Adriatic Bellflower grows best in humus-rich, sandy, well-drained soil. Space plants 12 inches apart in full sun. Where slugs are a problem, Bellflower is susceptible. Propagate plants from division or by seeds or cuttings. Mulch plants with pine boughs, straw, or hay in the colder limits of the hardiness range.

Cupid's Dart (*Catananche caerulea*)

The long-stalked blooms of Cupid's Dart are excellent for cutting and drying. Borne in summer, the 2-inch flowers bloom through the season on plants 2 feet tall. The very hairy, silvery-green leaves are mostly at the base of the plants. The variety 'Alba' has silvery-white flowers; 'Blue Giant' has large, pale blue flowers. Cupid's Dart is also called Blue Succory.

GROWING TIPS

Cupid's Dart grows in any ordinary garden soil that is well drained, especially in winter; it is tolerant of drought. Plant in full sun in groups of 3, spacing plants 12 inches apart. Seeds sown in early spring will flower the same year. Remove faded flowers to prolong the blooming season and to prevent invasive plants from self-sowing. Cupid's Dart is short-lived and needs dividing at least every other year. A winter mulch of pine boughs or straw is suggested for the colder areas of the hardiness range.

John Coutts Centaurea *(Centaurea hypoleuca)*   Zone 4

Graceful, fringed flowers, 2 inches across, bloom from early summer to midsummer on 18- to 24-inch plants. Pictured is the variety 'John Coutts'. The plants are useful in flower borders or for massed plantings, and the flowers are excellent for cutting. Seeds of the faded flowers attract birds to the garden. The deeply lobed leaves, more finely textured than the leaves of other centaureas, are silvery on the underside. Native to Turkey, the species is sometimes incorrectly identified as *C. dealbata*. Another centaurea, the Mountain Bluet *(C. montana)*, grows 18–24 inches tall with blue flowers.

GROWING TIPS

The John Coutts Centaurea survives neglect, even drought, if grown in well-drained, ordinary garden soil. Plant in groups of 3, spaced 12–18 inches apart in full sun. Remove faded flowers to prolong the blooming period. Division is necessary only about every 4 years.

Globe Centaurea *(Centaurea macrocephala)*

The showiest of the centaureas, Globe Centaurea bears thistle-like flower heads nearly 4 inches wide in early summer. These flowers attract butterflies and are excellent for drying. Native to Armenia, Globe Centaurea grows 3–4 feet tall with large, stiff leaves. A single plant toward the back of the flower border makes a bold statement.

GROWING TIPS

Globe Centaurea grows in ordinary, well-drained garden soil; drainage is especially important in winter. Plant in full sun. Staking may be necessary to keep plants upright when in bloom. If faded blooms are not removed, plants will readily self-sow. Plants can also be propagated by division in spring, usually only necessary every 4 years or so.

Red Valerian *(Centranthus ruber)*

The slender, spurred, ½-inch flowers of Red Valerian—also known as Jupiter's Beard—are borne in clusters during summer. These wonderfully fragrant blooms grow above blue- to gray-green foliage on plants 1–3 feet tall. Easily grown and a favorite garden plant, Red Valerian is a handsome addition to the middle of the flower border as well as along walls and limestone walks or outcroppings; the blossoms are also good cut flowers. The variety 'Albus' has white flowers; 'Atro-coccineus' has deep red flowers; and 'Roseus' has rose-red flowers.

GROWING TIPS

Red Valerian needs well-drained soil, especially in winter. Space plants 12–16 inches apart in full sun. If faded flowers are not removed, the plants will readily self-sow—the easiest way to get new plants. Dividing in the spring or taking cuttings in the early summer is also possible.

Pyrethrum *(Chrysanthemum coccineum)*

Pyrethrum, or Painted Daisy, is a popular summer-blooming perennial. The flower heads, often 2½ inches across, may be red, pink, lilac, or white; they are sometimes double. The bright green leaves, 1–3 feet tall, are finely divided and fernlike. There are many named forms, including 'Brenda', which is shown here.

GROWING TIPS

Pyrethrum needs moist, well-drained, humus-rich soil; soggy soil in winter will lessen its hardiness. Plant singly or in groups of 3, spacing 12–18 inches apart in full sun. Remove faded flowers to prolong the blooming season. Divide about every 4 years. Plant or divide in spring and mulch the following winter. Apply a light winter mulch of pine boughs or straw in the colder areas of the hardiness range.

Shasta Daisy *(Chrysanthemum × superbum)*

One of the most attractive and favored of perennial plants for the flower border, the Shasta Daisy blooms from early summer to midsummer. It is a superb flower for cutting, growing to 12–36 inches, with flower heads 2–4 inches across. There are dozens of different cultivars, varying not only in flower form but also plant height and hardiness. The variety 'Little Miss Muffet' is shown. There are also varieties with flowers with crested centers that resemble anemones, and full, shaggy double forms.

GROWING TIPS

Shasta Daisies need moist, humus-rich, well-drained soil; good drainage is crucial in winter. Plant singly or in groups of 3, spacing 12–18 inches apart. The single varieties are best in full sun, while the double need light shade. Plants are susceptible to verticillium rot, a fungus disease. Discard stricken plants immediately and do not replant chrysanthemums in the same place. Plants may need to be divided every other year, in spring. North of zone 5, provide a light winter mulch.

Lance Coreopsis *(Coreopsis lanceolata)* Zone 4

Both this species and Threadleaf Coreopsis *(C. verticillata)* are excellent plants for the low-maintenance garden. The long-lived Lance Coreopsis grows from 18–36 inches and bears 2-inch, daisylike flowers on wiry, graceful stems from early summer to midsummer. The leaves are narrow and light green. Threadleaf Coreopsis is somewhat smaller with very finely cut foliage. Some of the better known varieties of Lance Coreopsis include the compact 'Baby Sun' (pictured); 'Goldfink', with deep yellow blooms; and 'Sunray', with double gold blooms.

GROWING TIPS

Perennial coreopsis grows in any ordinary well-drained garden soil; moist, fertile soil causes plants to sprawl and increase rapidly. Plant in full sun. Threadleaf Coreopsis is particularly drought tolerant. Lance Coreopsis seldom needs dividing, and Threadleaf Coreopsis only about every 4 years; division may be done in spring or fall. Both types may also be propagated from seed; if sown in early spring, plants will bloom the first year.

Candle Larkspur *(Delphinium elatum)*

Among the most dramatic and desirable of garden flowers, delphiniums are also among the most finicky. When grown well, however, they are worth the effort. The bold flower spikes of the various hybrids—growing to 6 feet, in all shades of blue, purple, lavender, mauve, and white—may be single or double; some have a dark center called a "bee." Each individual flower may be 1–3 inches across. There are many widely available cultivars and hybrids.

GROWING TIPS

Delphiniums require humus-rich, moist soil that is fertilized regularly; a summer mulch is recommended. Space plants 24–30 inches apart. Areas of full sun protected from wind are best; plants do poorly in hot areas with long summers. Tall plants with heavy blossoms require staking; stakes should be in 12 inches of soil and rise to two-thirds the height of the stalk. Thin growth of established plants to the strongest 4 or 5 shoots. Divide every 3–4 years. Rebloom will often occur in fall if stalks are cut back.

Allwood Pink (*Dianthus* × *allwoodii*)

The neat tufts of blue-green foliage, 12–18 inches tall, of Allwood Pink are easily grown and long-lived. They are excellent for planting between paving stones in low-traffic areas, in the rock garden, or as an edging. The fragrant flowers, 1½–2 inches, are mostly semi-double, sometimes with fringed petals, in red, pink, white, or a combination. Plants bloom during the summer months.

GROWING TIPS

Allwood Pink grows in any ordinary garden soil that is extremely well drained and slightly alkaline, with some humus added. Space plants 8–12 inches apart in full sun. Cut off faded flowers. Divide plants every 2–3 years.

Grass Pink *(Dianthus plumarius)*

This mat-forming pink, growing 9–18 inches high, has smooth, blue-gray foliage. The fragrant flowers, 1½ inches across, may be rose-pink to purplish, white, or variegated, with fringed petals. Flowering occurs in late spring and early summer. Grass Pinks are excellent for the front of the flower border, as an edging, in dry stone walls, or in the rock garden. *Dianthus plumarius* var. *semperflorens* includes many common garden pinks with a long blooming season. Pictured is the cultivar 'Agatha'.

GROWING TIPS

Grass Pinks grow in any ordinary garden soil that is extremely well drained and slightly alkaline. Plant 8–12 inches apart in full sun. Prune plants after flowering. Plants are inclined to die out if left alone for 2–3 years, so keep your stock replenished through division, layering, or cuttings; all are easily managed since the plants root freely. A light mulch of evergreen branches reduces winter damage.

Purple Coneflower *(Echinacea purpurea)*

The bold and handsome Purple Coneflower, with its great masses of 3-inch flowers, makes a striking addition to the midsummer garden. Growing 2–4 feet tall with coarsely toothed leaves, it should be used in the middle to rear of the low-maintenance flower border. Cultivars include 'Alba', with creamy white flowers and copper-orange cones; 'Bright Star', with erect, lavender-pink petals around a dark cone; and 'Magnus', with broad, flaring petals of rosy purple around a shorter, dark cone. All are sometimes offered as *Brauneria*.

GROWING TIPS

Tolerant of drought and wind, Purple Coneflower is easily grown in well-drained, sandy loam soil. Space plants 15–18 inches apart in full sun to partial shade. Division is necessary only every 4 years or so. Plants are susceptible to Japanese beetle.

Globe Thistle (*Echinops ritro*)

An unusual plant, Globe Thistle grows 3–4 feet tall and has deeply cut, prickly leaves with white woolly undersides. The dense, spiny flower heads of metallic blue, 1½–2 inches across, readily attract bees to the garden during midsummer. Producing large clumps, they make a bold, showy statement in borders, among shrubs, or as specimen plants. The flowers are easily dried and used in winter arrangements. The cultivar 'Taplow Blue' is shown; other similar seed selections include 'Blue Globe', with deep blue, large flowers, and 'Veitch's Blue', with compact growth and smaller but more numerous flowers.

GROWING TIPS

Globe Thistle is easy to grow in any ordinary garden soil that is well drained; if soil is either too fertile or too moist, it tends to have floppy growth. Plant in full sun in groups of 3 at the middle or rear of the border, spacing plants 18–24 inches apart. Plants seldom need dividing, but can be increased by division as well as raised from seed.

Fleabane *(Erigeron)*

There are many colorful cultivars of fleabane, in shades of pink, violet, and lavender with yellow centers, that bloom during summer. The nearly stemless plants form spreading, dense tufts of leaves; when in flower, they grow to 18–24 inches tall. Fleabanes are best used in the front of the flower border or in rock gardens; 'Walther' is seen here. Other popular cultivars include 'Double Beauty', with double violet to blue flowers; 'Foerster's Darling', extra hardy plants with double pink flowers; 'Pink Jewel', with large, single pink flowers; and 'Prosperity', with semidouble, mauve-blue flowers. All are excellent for cutting.

GROWING TIPS

Fleabane is easy to grow in any well-drained garden soil that is relatively dry, sandy, and infertile. It grows best in maritime climates, but will tolerate hot summers if given light shade at midday. Plant in groups of at least 3, spacing plants 12–15 inches apart, in full sun. Remove faded flowers to prolong blooming. Divide in spring every 4 years.

Zabel Eryngo (*Eryngium × zabelii*)

Also known as Sea Holly, these are very striking, handsome plants with spiny-edged leaves and unusual flowers. They are easy to grow; the plants, growing to 2–2½ feet, provide a bold effect in the flower border. The long-lived Zabel Eryngo is probably a hybrid of *E. alpinium* and *E. bourgatii*. The 1-inch flowers, steel gray shading to amethyst, are produced in summer. The related Mediterranean Eryngo (*E. bourgatii*), grows 24 inches tall, with round, stiff leaves marked with white veins, and ¾-inch blue-and-white flower heads in midsummer.

Use eryngo in the middle of the flower border or rock garden; the flowers are excellent for cutting, both fresh and dried.

GROWING TIPS

Eryngo thrive in well-drained sandy soil of moderate to low fertility; Zabel Eryngo is more tolerant of clay-loam soils than the others. Plant singly or in pairs, 12–16 inches apart, in full sun. Because of the deep, fleshy roots, they do not transplant well. Root cuttings are the best means of propagation.

Cushion Spurge (*Euphorbia epithymoides*) Zone 5

Often listed in catalogues as *E. polychroma,* Cushion Spurge forms a neat, cushion-shaped, roundish clump about 12 inches high. In spring, plants are covered with showy, chartreuse-yellow bracts an inch wide. The actual flowers are greenish, small, and in a dense cluster. In the fall, leaves turn red. Use Cushion Spurge at the front of the flower border, in the rock garden, or among tulips. The bracts and flowers of all euphorbias are long-lasting when cut, but have a milky sap that may cause an allergic reaction; keep plant away from eyes, mouth, and open cuts. To keep the milky sap from running out, char the cut ends of the stem with a match, then plunge into water.

GROWING TIPS

Plant in full sun. Cushion Spurge is easily grown in dry, well-drained garden soil, but will not thrive in hot, humid climates. Plants are long-lived but do not transplant well. Seldom bothered by pests. Propagate by division.

Euphorbia *(Euphorbia griffithii)*

The showy bracts of the euphorbia cultivar 'Fire Glow', seen here, bloom in early summer. The flower clusters reach 2–4 inches across. The 3-foot plants have long, narrow leaves with pale pink midribs. In the fall, the leaves turn red. This plant makes a good cut flower, and may be used in bouquets. When broken or cut, the plant releases a milky sap that may cause an allergic reaction; keep sap away from eyes, mouth, and open cuts. To prevent the sap from running, char the cut ends with a match before plunging into water.

Growing Tips

Fire Glow Euphorbia is easy to grow in dry, well-drained garden soil of ordinary fertility. Plant in full sun to partial shade. Plants are long-lived but do not transplant well. They are seldom bothered by pests. Propagate by division.

Blanketflower *(Gaillardia × grandiflora)*

Blooming throughout the summer months, Blanketflower is a bright, colorful addition to the flower border. Plants grow 8–36 inches high, depending on the variety, and have slightly hairy leaves; the flowers are usually 3–4 inches across. The lower-growing forms do well in rock gardens as well as borders. Two of the most popular cultivars include 'Baby Cole', growing 10–12 inches tall with brilliant yellow flowers with maroon centers, and 'Burgundy', growing 30 inches tall with 3-inch, wine-red flowers.

GROWING TIPS

The drought-tolerant Blanketflower needs light, open, well-drained soil. It will not survive in heavy, wet soils during winter. Space plants 12–15 inches apart in full sun. The crown in the center of the plant often dies; as new flowers appear away from the crown, those plants can be dug up and transplanted. If planted from seed, Blanketflower often flowers in the first year.

Goat's Rue (*Galega officinalis*)

Forming a large, loose clump 2–3 feet tall, Goat's Rue bears spikes of pealike, ½-inch flowers, in pink, white, or purplish throughout the summer. The leaflets are featherlike. There are forms with all-white flowers and bicolored, lilac-blue, and white blossoms; one form has variegated leaves.

GROWING TIPS

Goat's Rue grows well in average soil. Space plants 18 inches apart in full sun to partial shade. Staking or other support may be required. Cut back plants when flowering is finished to keep plants from crowding others. Propagate from seed or by division in the spring.

White Gaura (*Gaura lindheimeri*)

A pretty species native to Louisiana and Texas, the White Gaura grows 3–5 feet tall with slender, branching stems and small, narrow leaves. The name gaura is derived from *gauros,* for "superb," in reference to the beauty of the flowers. When they first appear, the blooms are white, but they soon change to light pink; ½–1 inch across, they are borne on erect, wandlike stalks from early summer to fall.

GROWING TIPS

Start plants from seed, spacing them 12 inches apart in full sun. White Gaura is very easy to grow in any ordinary garden soil, provided that the soil is well drained. In poorly drained areas, raise the bed. Gaura has a long taproot and needs watering only in the driest part of summer. North of zone 7, provide a winter mulch.

Blood-red Cranesbill *(Geranium sanguineum)*   Zone 4

Forming spreading mounds 12–18 inches high, with attractive starry leaves, Blood-red Cranesbill is the best of the hardy geraniums for the flower border. Plants bloom in great profusion from late spring to midsummer, and sometimes repeat. The reddish-purple to pale pink flowers are 1 inch wide. Pictured is the variety *lancastriense,* also known as *prostratum* or *striatum;* it grows about 6 inches tall and has light pink flowers veined in crimson. There is also a white-flowered variety. Use Blood-red Cranesbill and its varieties in the rock garden, as an edging or ground cover, or in the front of the flower border. Others to consider include *G. dalmaticum* and Pyrenean Cranesbill *(G. endressii).*

GROWING TIPS

Blood-red Cranesbill is the most adaptable of the cranesbills, tolerating hot, dry summers. Set plants 8–14 inches apart in full sun, in moist, well-drained garden soil. Readily increased by division of clumps in the spring or from seed; division is usually only necessary about every 4 years.

Chilean Avens *(Geum quellyon)*

Compound, deeply cut, or lobed leaves form ground-hugging clumps from which arise 24-inch slender stalks bearing flowers singly or in clusters. Up to 1½ inches across, the single or double, summer-blooming flowers of Chilean Avens may be orange, red, or yellow. This plant may also be sold as *G. chiloense*. Cultivars include 'Borisii', a hardier hybrid growing 12–18 inches tall, and 'Mrs. Bradshaw' (pictured), with brick-red semidouble flowers. The related Avens, *Geum reptans,* grows 6–8 inches high with 1½-inch flowers.

GROWING TIPS

Avens are easy to grow in moist, humus-rich, well-drained soil. Soggy soil in winter will be fatal. Grow in full sun to partial shade, spacing plants 12–18 inches apart, in groups of 3. Plants are slow to become established and division is seldom necessary. Remove faded flowers before seeds form to prolong bloom into fall. Mulch in winter in northern limits of hardiness.

Tatarian Statice (*Goniolimon tataricum*)

An indispensable flower for dried arrangements, Tatarian Statice is also an excellent dwarf plant for the front of the flower border. The lance-shaped leaves form a ground-hugging rosette. During summer, large masses of the narrowly winged flower branches grow about 18 inches tall with ¼-inch rosy-pink flowers. After the petals fade and drop, the calyx—white with green veins—remains; it is this stage that is used dried in craft projects and bouquets. Native to southern Europe, Tatarian Statice is closely related to Sea-lavender and Annual Statice, both members of the genus *Limonium;* Tatarian Statice is sometimes listed as *Limonium tatarica.*

GROWING TIPS

Easy to grow in full sun in most well-drained garden soils. Space plants 12–16 inches apart. Since it takes several years for plants to become established, do not divide or transplant unless absolutely necessary. It is propagated from seed or root cuttings.

Baby's-Breath (*Gypsophila*)

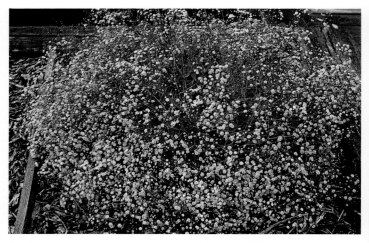

The airy, fine-textured, profusely produced flowers of gypsophilas have long endeared them to gardeners for their effect in the garden as well as in fresh and dried bouquets. The species *G. paniculata*, pictured, grows 3 feet tall and as wide, with numerous ¼-inch flowers in spring and summer. The most popular cultivar is 'Bristol Fairy', with double flowers produced from summer into fall, if faded flowers are removed. Creeping Baby's-Breath (*G. repens*) grows 6–8 inches tall, with flowers ¼ inch across on 12- to 18-inch stems.

Growing Tips

Baby's-breath needs well-drained, neutral to slightly alkaline garden soil. Plants will not survive soggy soil in winter. Plant in full sun in spring, spacing plants 24–36 inches apart; space Creeping Baby's-Breath 12–18 inches apart. It will take 2 years before plants become fully established, and baby's-breath should not be moved once planted. Named varieties are grafted onto roots; set this graft union 1 inch below the soil line. Stake tall-growing types.

False Sunflower *(Helenium autumnale)*

Well suited to the middle or rear of the informal flower border or as part of the meadow garden, False Sunflower is a bright addition to the fall color palette. Growing to 5 feet high, the large flower stems bear great numbers of 2-inch flowers of yellow, orange, or mahogany with darker centers. Blooming starts in late summer and continues into fall. The flowers are particularly long-lasting when cut for bouquets. Recommended cultivars include 'Brilliant', growing to 3 feet, and 'Moerheim Beauty', with deep bronze-red flowers.

GROWING TIPS

False Sunflower needs fertile, humus-rich, moist soil; it does not tolerate drought. Grow in full sun, singly or in groups of 3, spacing plants 18 inches apart. Divide plants in the spring every 2–3 years to propagate and keep them looking tidy. Taller-growing types may need staking or pinching back in the spring to make the growth more compact.

Rock Rose *(Helianthemum nummularium)*

The low, spreading, woody branches of the evergreen Rock Rose are an ideal addition to the rock garden, on steep banks, or the front of the flower border. Growing 9–12 inches high, the creeping plants bear thin-petalled 1-inch flowers in early summer. When faded flowers are removed, plants will bloom again in autumn. The blooms open in early morning and close up by noon. Colors include yellow, orange, red, pink, and white. 'Fire Dragon' is seen here.

GROWING TIPS

Rock Rose grows best in well-drained, sandy, alkaline soil. Space plants 12–18 inches apart in full sun. Prune back plants in the spring to keep plants from becoming straggly. Plants are slow to establish, so divide and transplant only when absolutely necessary. Cuttings taken in early summer readily root. Mulch lightly with straw or evergreen branches in winter in the more northern areas of the plant's hardiness range.

Perennial Sunflower *(Helianthus × multiflorus)* Zone 5

These bold, bright plants grow to 6 feet high with slightly hairy, coarsely toothed leaves. In summer the plants are crowned with flower heads to 5 inches across, which are splendid for cutting. 'Flore Pleno' is a double form that resembles a dahlia. Perennial Sunflower is excellent for the back of the flower border, in large clumps as an accent in the landscape, or naturalized in meadow gardens or along the edge of a wood. The related Swamp Sunflower *(H. angustifolius),* is not as hardy. It bears shiny, narrow leaves and 2- to 3-inch yellow flowers with purple centers in late summer. Growing 6 feet high, it tolerates both wet and dry soils.

GROWING TIPS

Perennial Sunflower requires full sun and grows best in moist, deep, humus-rich, fertile soil. Space plants 12–24 inches apart. Enrich the soil each year in spring with compost or manure. Plants may need dividing every year.

False Sunflower *(Heliopsis helianthoides)*

Growing 3–4 feet tall, with rough-textured leaves that are rather coarsely toothed, False Sunflower is useful for informal flower borders or wild gardens. Blooming for a long period in late summer, the flower heads are 1½–2½ inches across; they are very good cut for arrangements. Durable and showy, False Sunflower readily naturalizes and does not need staking. The variety *scabra* (Orange Sunflower, pictured) bears orange-yellow blooms; 'Summer Sun' has double, large yellow blossoms.

GROWING TIPS

False Sunflower is easy to grow in moist, humus-rich, average soil. Plant in full sun, 12–24 inches apart. Plants can be propagated by seeds, cuttings, or division of the roots. Adding humus to the soil will help growth.

Daylily *(Hemerocallis)*

One of the most popular and best performing flowers for any garden, daylilies add color and grace to flower borders. They can also be allowed to naturalize on slopes, along paths, or interplanted with shrubs and other garden plants. There are thousands of hybrids available in every color except blue and true white. Most are grown as bulbs, but there are forms that work well as perennials. The flowers are funnel form or bell shaped, 2–8 inches wide, with a single or double row of petals; they are borne in clusters on long, thin stalks. Each bloom lasts only a day, but many are produced over time. Find cultivars that flower in spring, summer, or fall, for season-long color. 'Admiral Nelson' is pictured.

GROWING TIPS

Daylilies are practically indestructible, and they grow in any reasonably fertile, moist, well-drained garden soil. Plant in full sun in the spring or fall, spacing plants 18–24 inches apart. Older types seldom need dividing, but the newer ones do better if divided every 3–6 years.

Rose Mallow (*Hibiscus moscheutos*) Zone 5

Bearing some of the largest flowers of any perennial, the Rose Mallow is a spectacular, tropical-looking sight in the garden. It blooms throughout most of the summer, bearing flowers 4–7 inches across; early in the season, these blooms can grow to 12 inches. Colors include white as well as shades of pink and red; many hybrids are available. The leaves are large and gray-green, and the plants grow 3–8 feet high. Use Rose Mallow in a large flower border, among shrubs, or massed. Flowers are not good for cutting as they wilt within an hour.

GROWING TIPS
Rose Mallow is very easy to grow in any ordinary garden soil, tolerating average to very moist conditions. Space plants 24 inches apart in full sun. Plants are long-lived and should not be disturbed; although they grow large, they die down to the ground in winter and start new growth very late in spring. Susceptible to Japanese Beetles. Mulch plants with straw or pine boughs in areas with winter temperatures of 0° F or colder.

Candytuft (*Iberis sempervirens*)

With its mounds of shiny evergreen leaves, growing to 12 inches high and up to 24 inches across, Candytuft provides an attractive edging for a flower border or path. It is also excellent for rock gardens. From mid-spring to late spring, Candytuft is covered with finger-shaped flower clusters, each about 1½ inches across. Varieties include 'Autumn Snow', which blooms again in fall; 'Bluemont Snow', which blooms very early; and 'Little Gem', a compact, very fine-leaved variety, 6 inches high and 8 inches across.

GROWING TIPS

Candytuft is a low-maintenance perennial for full sun. It grows best in a moist, well-drained, light, moderately fertile soil. In flower borders, plant in groups of 3 or more, spaced 12–15 inches apart; as an edging, space 8–12 inches apart, depending on the size of the variety. It seldom needs dividing. To prevent plants from becoming straggly and open in the middle, cut back stems halfway after flowering. Propagate from cuttings taken in the fall. Mulch in winter with pine boughs in cold areas without much snow.

Swordleaf Inula *(Inula ensifolia)*

Easy to grow, Swordleaf Inula is a good plant for the front of the flower border. In midsummer, the 12-inch plants, with hairy, slightly curled leaves, bear 1½-inch yellow flowers. In cool climates, flowering continues for over a month; where temperatures are higher, this period is shorter. The variety 'Compacta' grows 8 inches tall. The related Oriental Inula *(Inula orientalis)* grows 2 feet high with 3-inch, orange-yellow flowers.

GROWING TIPS

Swordleaf Inula thrives in moist, well-drained garden soil of average fertility. Space plants 12–18 inches apart in full sun; plants may also be started from seed, and if sown early enough, will bloom the first year. Remove faded flowers to prolong blooming period. Mildew may be a problem.

Japanese Iris *(Iris ensata)*

The Japanese Iris is one of the most stunning of all perennials, and the source of many intensely colored varieties in shades of blue-violet, purple, blue, lavender, red-purple, mahogany red, pink or white. Some varieties are marked with a contrasting color. All have the bright yellow signal marks on the center of the petals. Pictured is the variety 'Azure'. The flat blooms may be up to 6 inches across; they appear from midsummer to late summer with 2–4 flowers on each 3- to 4-foot stem. The narrow, sword-shaped leaves reach 2–3 feet.

GROWING TIPS

Japanese Iris have very exacting growing requirements. The soil must be acid, fertile, humus-rich, and very moist during the growing season. Lime placed anywhere near them will cause fatalities. Plant in spring in full sun to partial shade at streamsides or pond margins, spacing plants 10–16 inches apart and setting the crown 2 inches deep. Japanese Iris need dividing about every 3–4 years. Cover with evergreen boughs where winters are colder than −10°F.

Bearded Iris (*Iris*)

Old-fashioned perennial favorites, the many cultivars of Bearded Iris are exquisitely shaded in nearly every possible color; there are also bicolored cultivars, as well as ones with petals edged in a contrasting color. Bloom varies from mid-spring to late spring; flowers are excellent for cutting. Bearded Iris range in height from 16 inches to over 3 feet, depending on the variety; it has 6 petals—3 erect and 3 falling, and the outer segments are usually 2–3 inches long.

GROWING TIPS

Bearded Iris are easily grown in any moderately fertile, moist, well-drained garden soil. Set rhizomes 1 inch deep in full sun, spaced 10–16 inches apart, with the fan of leaves pointing in the direction you want the plant to grow. Remove faded flowers to prevent seed formation. Divide clumps about every 3–4 years. After flowering is finished, dig up and separate the rhizomes and trim back the leaves to 6 inches. Replant in groups of 3.

Red-hot Poker *(Kniphofia uvaria)*

The flamelike spikes of Red-hot Poker or Torch Lily bloom over a long period in summer. Early-blooming varieties will rebloom in fall. The unusual flowers, composed of drooping florets, 1½–2 inches long, are borne in spikelike clusters 6–12 inches long. The thin, grasslike leaves form dense clumps 2–4 feet high and 2–3 feet wide. Hybrids are available in both soft and bright shades, including coral-red, yellow, cream, salmon, and red. Plant singly or in groups of 3. Plants may be listed as *Tritoma* in catalogues.

GROWING TIPS

Red-hot Poker needs fertile, humus-rich, moist but perfectly drained soil; it must be sheltered from strong winds. Space plants 15–18 inches apart in full sun. It may take several years for plants to become established and attain some size. Remove faded flowers to encourage reblooming. Plant or divide only in the spring. Mulch with straw or evergreen boughs in areas with a minimum winter temperature of 0° F or colder, or tie leaves into a canopy-like bundle to protect the crown.

Lavender *(Lavandula angustifolia)*

Zones 5–6

One of the most beloved of the old-fashioned fragrant plants, Lavender bears delicately scented spikes of pale or dark purple flowers 1–3 feet high. Each individual flower is about ⅓ inch long. Plants bloom throughout summer, especially if flower stems are cut off. The gray-green foliage, 2 inches long or less, is very narrow and densely white-felty. Lavender makes an excellent low-growing hedge in milder climates; otherwise use it in flower borders and rock and herb gardens. Plants may also be listed as *L. officinalis* or *L. vera*.

GROWING TIPS

Lavender grows best in full sun in well-drained, sandy, neutral soil. Soil that is too fertile will reduce hardiness. Remove flower spikes to encourage reblooming. Prune back the old wood in the spring to force new growth. Propagate by division or cuttings; the species may also be started from seed. Mulch with evergreen boughs in areas with winter minimum temperatures of 0° F.

Sea-lavender *(Limonium latifolium)*

The leathery, deep green, oval leaves of Sea-lavender, 6–9 inches long, form a ground-hugging evergreen rosette. In summer, many-branched stems, 18–24 inches long, are covered with tiny flowers. Plants may be up to 36 inches across with a dozen stems when in full bloom. Native to salt marshes, Sea-lavender is resistant to salt spray. Use toward the front of the flower border or in the rock garden. The stems dry readily for use in winter arrangements; simply cut the stems when flowers are fully open and hang upside down in a dark, airy place. There are pink-flowered and deep violet-blue forms. Plants may be listed as statice.

GROWING TIPS

Sea-lavender is easy to grow in sandy, moist soil. If grown in heavy clay soil, stems will be weak and need to be staked. Space plants 12–16 inches apart in full sun. The long roots require a deep planting hole; division or transplanting should be infrequent.

Golden Flax *(Linum flavum)*

Long-lived and requiring only minimal maintenance, Golden Flax provides a cheery effect in the front to middle of the flower border; its 1-inch yellow flowers are especially suited to the rock garden. The related Perennial Flax *(L. perenne)* has fine-textured, feathery foliage and graceful stems. Although its 1-inch flowers last only a day, they bloom profusely along the stems throughout the summer. There are varieties with white, sapphire-blue, or red flowers as well as compact growth. Both reach 1–2 feet.

GROWING TIPS

Golden Flax and Perennial Flax are easily grown in any light, well-drained garden soil. Soggy soil in winter will decrease hardiness. Space plants 10–14 inches apart in full sun. Propagate by division or by cuttings.

German Catchfly *(Lychnis viscaria)*

Blooming from late spring to early summer, German Catchfly grows in dense clumps of grassy, evergreen foliage, about 12 inches high; it bears bunches of fragrant, double, ½-inch flowers on the 18-inch stems. Seen here is the cultivar 'Splendens Plena'. Other cultivars include white-, red-, and pink-flowered forms as well as a dwarf variety growing 4 inches high. Use German Catchfly in flower borders, the rock garden, and for cut flowers. The related Maltese Cross *(L. chalcedonica)* grows 18–30 inches high with dense clusters of 1-inch scarlet flowers in midsummer. Rose Campion *(L. coronaria)* has woolly, silvery-gray leaves and 1-inch magenta flowers on 2-foot stems; plants are short-lived but readily self-sow.

GROWING TIPS

German Catchfly is easy to grow in any moist, well-drained garden soil. Space plants 10–18 inches apart in sun or partial shade. Propagate by division in spring.

Purple Loosestrife (*Lythrum salicaria*)

Purple Loosestrife has willowlike leaves on plants 2–6 feet high. From midsummer to late summer, plants bear densely-covered spikes of pink or bright purple flowers, ¾ inch wide. A marsh plant, the species has naturalized throughout much of North America because it readily self-sows; in some areas, it has become an invasive weed. In the garden, use of cultivars is recommended as they are less aggressive. Some popular cultivars are the rich purple 'Dropmore Purple'; the rose-red 'Firecandle'; 'Happy', with pink flowers on short, 15-inch plants; 'Pink Spires', with rich, deep pink, sterile flowers; and 'Robert', with rose-red flowers. Use Purple Loosestrife in flower borders, along ponds and streams, or in large drifts.

GROWING TIPS

Purple Loosestrife grows best near streams or pools, although it will also work in open borders. Space plants 12–18 inches apart in full sun. Propagate by division, cuttings, or seeds.

Musk Mallow *(Malva moschata)*

The delicate, 2-inch, crêpelike flowers of the Musk Mallow appear in the upper leaf axils from mid- to late summer. The white form, 'Alba', is seen here; there is also a form with pink flowers. Foliage is hairy and finely divided; stems grow 1–3 feet tall. Musk Mallow can be used in the middle to rear of the flower border. The Hollyhock Mallow *(M. alcea)* grows 2 feet tall with deep pink flowers.

GROWING TIPS

Musk Mallow is easy to grow in any ordinary, well-drained garden soil, but prefers dry soil in sun to partial shade. Space plants 16–24 inches apart. Propagate by division in spring or fall or from seeds started in early spring.

Mauve Catmint (Nepeta mussinii)

The heart-shaped, gray-green leaves and spikes of ¼-inch flowers make Mauve Catmint an attractive plant, and its low, spreading growth makes it an excellent edging plant or accent for the front of the flower border. The soft color combines particularly well with pink-flowered plants. The foliage has a pungent scent that some people find pleasing. Growing 12 inches high and sprawling to 3 feet across, Mauve Catmint blooms profusely from early summer to mid-summer, and sporadically until fall. A sterile hybrid, N. × faassenii, grows 18 inches high with lavender-blue flowers; it is a more attractive ground cover.

GROWING TIPS

Catmint is easy to grow in sandy, well-drained soil. Space plants 12 inches apart in full sun. Cut back stems by about half after the first blooming to increase the fall bloom and encourage bushy growth. The species may be propagated from seed sown in spring or summer; cultivars are increased by division or sometimes from the runners.

Missouri Primrose *(Oenothera missourensis)*   Zone 5

Also called Ozark Sundrops, this native flower is an adaptable, long-lived plant excellent for the front of the flower border. Trailing branches, 3–6 inches long, bear saucer-shaped, upward-facing flowers to 7 inches long and 4 inches across. These lightly fragrant blooms open in the evening and remain open until the end of the next day. Flowering continues on this garden favorite from early summer to midsummer. As flowers fade, large, winged seedpods develop. The foliage turns reddish in the fall. The Showy Primrose *(O. speciosa)* is a slightly sprawling plant growing 6–18 inches tall with day-blooming, 2-inch, white or pink flowers; it has a tendency to spread and become a pest. The Common Sundrop *(O. tetragona)* grows 18 inches high with bright yellow flowers.

GROWING TIPS

Oenothera are easy to grow in any sunny spot with sandy or loamy, well-drained soil. Space plants 12 inches apart. Division, seldom necessary, may be done in early spring. Plants can also be started from seed.

Peony *(Paeonia)*

Peonies are a popular favorite because they are attractive, long-lived, and require little maintenance. They bloom in late spring to early summer, and may have single, semidouble, or double flowers 3–12 inches across. Colors range from white to many different shades of pink and red, often with golden stamens in the center; there is 1 species with yellow flowers. The relatively large, handsome leaves are composed of divided leaflets. The Chinese, or Common, Peony *(P. lactiflora)* grows 2–3 feet high with flowers 3–5 inches across; the hor-ticultural variety 'Ms. Wilder Bancroft' is pictured. The Common Peony *(P. officinalis)* grows to 3 feet high with 4-inch flowers.

GROWING TIPS

Peonies need a deep, humus-rich, fertile, moist but well-drained soil. Set buds, or "eyes," 1–1½ inches below the soil surface in full sun to partial shade; deeper planting will inhibit flowering. Space plants 3 feet apart. Plants should not be transplanted or divided unless absolutely necessary.

Oriental Poppy *(Papaver orientale)*

The sheer, 6-inch blooms of Oriental Poppy come in luminescent shades of red, pink, salmon, and white, often marked with contrasting colors at the edge of the petals and in the center. The plants grow 3–4 feet high and 2–3 feet across, with coarse, hairy leaves. Any part of the plant, if cut or broken, exudes a milky substance; to use poppies as cut flowers, sear the cut end in a flame. After flowering, the plants become dormant, so interplant with broad-growing perennials. The cultivar 'China Boy' is seen here.

GROWING TIPS

Oriental Poppies are easy to grow in full sun in ordinary, well-drained garden soil; drainage is vital in winter, when standing water will cause the greatest damage. Place the roots 3 inches below the soil surface and space plants 18–24 inches apart. Plants may need staking when in flower. Divide or transplant poppies in late summer or early fall; they should be mulched lightly in the winter. It takes about 2 years for transplants to bloom.

Gloxinia Penstemon *(Penstemon gloxinioides)*   Zone 9

Also known as Beardtongue, Gloxinia Penstemon bears 2-inch flowers of white, blue, or crimson, that resemble foxglove *(Digitalis)*. This is actually a group of cultivars, including 'Firebird' and 'Garnet'; they are very popular on the West Coast and in England; they may be grown as annuals in cold climates. Other penstemons are hardier and somewhat longer-lived. The Beardlip Penstemon (*P. barbatus,* hardy to zone 4) has 1-inch, bearded red flowers; well-known cultivars include 'Rose Elf' and 'Prairie Fire'. *Penstemon hirsutus,* hardy to zone 5, has hairy, sticky stems with purple or violet flowers 1 inch wide. All penstemons grow 2–3 feet high with evergreen leaves at the base; they bloom from late spring to midsummer.

GROWING TIPS
Penstemons are easily grown in any ordinary, well-drained garden soil; they like full sun, but may be longer-lived if given partial shade. Space plants 8–12 inches apart. Readily divided or started from seed. Mulch lightly in winter.

Azure Sage (Perovskia atriplicifolia)

From midsummer to late summer, clouds of ¼-inch tubular flowers form feathery plumes on Azure Sage. The shrubby plants grow 3–5 feet tall with semi-woody, silver-gray stems. The small, toothed leaves are covered with grayish-white hairs and have a sagelike odor. Native to central Asia, Azure Sage is an excellent cut flower as well as an attractive, airy addition to the flower border.

GROWING TIPS

Azure Sage is easy to grow in well-drained garden soil. Space plants 18–30 inches apart in full sun. Cut plants to the ground each spring to promote strong growth and maximum flowering. Propagate by summer cuttings. North of zone 6, apply a light winter mulch of straw or evergreen boughs.

Balloon Flower (*Platycodon grandiflorus*)

This handsome border plant blooms throughout the summer until frost. In bud, the 5 petals look like inflated balloons; they open to 2- to 3-inch, saucer-shaped flowers. The oval to long, narrow leaves are dark green. Plants form long-lived, compact clumps. Because it is slow to emerge in the spring, mark its location to prevent accidentally digging it up during spring clean-up. Flower stems are good for cutting if the cut ends are seared with a flame. There are various colors, including dark violet-blue, white, and pink, as well as double blue flowers.

GROWING TIPS

Balloon Flower is easy to grow in light, well-drained soil of average fertility. Use in groups of 3 in sun to partial shade, spacing about 15 inches apart. Increase by division in the spring or from seed. Plants take 2 years to flower when grown from seed; even divisions are slow to become established and should not be moved unless absolutely necessary. Plant support may be needed with taller-growing varieties.

Cinquefoil (*Potentilla*)

Somewhat resembling wild strawberry *(Fragaria)*, cinquefoils have leaves composed of 3 hairy leaflets, and either creeping or erect stems. The flowers have 5 red, yellow, or white petals. Ruby Cinquefoil *(P. atrosanguinea)* grows 12–18 inches high with loose clusters of 1-inch red flowers; 'Gibson's Scarlet', the variety shown, has single red flowers. Nepal Cinquefoil *(P. nepalensis)* grows to 2 feet high with long-stalked, branching clusters of 1-inch, rose-red flowers; 'Roxana' has pink, orange, and red-brown flowers. Sulphur Cinquefoil *(P. recta,* to zone 4) has flowering stems 2 feet high with 1-inch yellow flowers; it does well in hot areas. Spring Cinquefoil *(P. tabernaemontana)* grows 3 inches high, with ½-inch yellow flowers.

GROWING TIPS

Most cinquefoils grow well in dry, well-drained soil. Space plants 10–18 inches apart in full sun. They should be divided every 3 years, in early spring or early fall; they may also be started from seed sown in sandy soil.

Deer Grass *(Rhexia virginica)*

A pretty little native of sandy bogs along the coast of eastern North America, Deer Grass grows 9–18 inches high with hairy-fringed, prominently veined leaves. The 1½-inch flowers bloom from summer to early fall in small clusters. The related Maryland Meadowbeauty *(R. mariana)* is a slender plant of pine-barren bogs growing 1–2 feet high. The pale purple flowers, appearing in small clusters, are 1½ inches wide.

GROWING TIPS

Deer Grass and Maryland Meadowbeauty are easy to grow in moist, acid, boggy soil. Space plants 12 inches apart in full sun. They should not be moved very often, but can be increased by lifting clumps in fall or spring, carefully separating, then replanting.

Orange Coneflower *(Rudbeckia fulgida)*   Zone 4

Resembling our native Black-eyed Susans *(R. hirta),* Orange Coneflowers have daisylike flower heads, 3 inches wide, with outer petals a bright orange-yellow and a black center. The variety *speciosa* has flower heads to 4 inches wide with yellow petals and a brown-purple center. These grow 2 to 3 feet tall. The cultivar 'Goldsturm' is a compact, well-branched form 2 feet high with 3- to 4-inch flowers that bloom from midsummer until frost. It is one of the best of all low-maintenance perennials. *Rudbeckia nitida* 'Herbstsonne' (also listed as 'Autumn Sun') grows 4–7 feet high and has high-centered, 4-inch flowers from midsummer to late summer. All types are excellent as cut flowers.

GROWING TIPS

Coneflowers are easy to grow in moist or average well-drained garden soil of moderate fertility; good winter drainage is necessary. Grow the species from seed, but the cultivars should be grown from root divisions in early spring. In spring, space plants 12–15 inches apart in full sun in groups of 3 or more.

Lavender Cotton *(Santolina chamaecyparissus)* Zone 6

A neat-looking, silvery-gray evergreen mound growing 1–2 feet high, Lavender Cotton has feathery, finely cut leaves and blooms from midsummer to late summer. The globe-shaped flower heads, ¾-inch wide, are borne singly on 6-inch stalks. Plants may also be sold as *S. incana*. Green Lavender Cotton (*S. virens*) has smooth, dark, very narrow, 2-inch long, evergreen foliage. Plants grow in mounds 10–18 inches high. The ½-inch creamy yellow flowers are on stout stalks 6–10 inches tall. Both kinds have aromatic foliage and can be used singly or in groups, massed as a ground cover, especially on banks.

GROWING TIPS

Lavender Cotton grows best in well-drained soil in full sun. Space plants 12 inches apart. Cut back plants in early spring to prevent them from becoming ragged. Remove faded flowers. Propagate in summer from stem cuttings. Mulch lightly with evergreen boughs where winter temperatures drop below 0° F; north of zone 6, treat as an annual.

94 PERENNIALS FOR SUN

Rock Soapwort *(Saponaria ocymoides)*

The trailing, semi-evergreen plants, 4–8 inches high, of Rock Soapwort are excellent for training over rock walls or as an edging or ground cover. The brightly colored, ½-inch flowers are borne in loose clusters from late spring to early summer. There is also a white-flowered variety as well as one called 'Rubra Compacta', which has more brilliant, deeper pink flowers and compact growth. A related plant is Bouncing Bet, or Soapwort *(S. officinalis)*, growing 1–3 feet high with pink or white, 1-inch flowers in dense clusters in summer. It blooms mostly at night and can be invasive in moist, fertile soil. The variety *flore-pleno,* with double flowers, is the form usually grown.

GROWING TIPS

Saponarias are easy to grow in full sun in average, well-drained soil. They are easy to propagate from seeds in early spring, by division of rootstocks in early spring or fall, or by cuttings. Insert cuttings in a balanced mixture of sand and soil, and provide shade until rooted.

Pincushion Flower *(Scabiosa caucasica)*

Pincushion Flower is an excellent low-maintenance perennial as well as a good cut flower. It blooms for a long period during summer into fall. The flowers may be in shades of blue or white and 2–3 inches across; bristling with stamens, they grow on stems to 2½ feet tall. The oval or lance-shaped leaves are often lobed or deeply cut. The cultivar 'David Wilkie', pictured, has pinkish-purple flowers. All are relatively free of pests.

GROWING TIPS

Pincushion Flower is easy to grow in moist, neutral to alkaline, well-drained soil. Plant in full sun in groups of 3 or more, spaced 12–15 inches apart. Propagate in very early spring by seeds or division.

Aizoon Stonecrop *(Sedum aizoon)*

Strong-growing, with upright stems 12–18 inches high, Aizoon Stonecrop bears clusters of star-shaped yellow flowers, ½ inch across, during summer. The blooms, which attract butterflies, are followed by colorful red seed capsules. The foliage is dark green and succulent, with bronze-red stems. Another sedum in the same color range is the Orange Stonecrop (*S. kamtschaticum*). It has orange-yellow, ¾-inch flowers in midsummer. The succulent, deep green leaves have scalloped edges; a varie-gated kind has leaves edged in cream. Plants have upright stems 6–12 inches high. Both are excellent for the front of the border or the rock garden; Orange Stonecrop will also grow in partial shade.

GROWING TIPS

Aizoon Stonecrop needs sandy, humus-enriched soil and full sun. Space plants 12 inches apart. Good drainage is essential, particularly in winter. Propagate by seeds, division, cuttings, or leaves.

Showy Stonecrop (*Sedum spectabile*)

Indispensable to the low-maintenance garden and nearly indestructible, Showy Stonecrop grows 18–24 inches high and bears succulent, gray-green leaves. The clusters of ½-inch star-shaped flowers, blooming in late summer to fall, are 3–4 inches wide. Cultivars include 'Brilliant', a raspberry-red; 'Meteor', a deep red; 'Carmen', a soft rose-pink; 'Star Dust', an ivory; and 'Variegatum', with red flowers and variegated leaves. 'Autumn Joy', a hybrid between *S. spectabile* and *S. telephium,* is among the best of all perennials.

GROWING TIPS

Showy Stonecrop and related types are easy to grow in well-drained garden soil. Good drainage is essential, particularly in winter. Space plants 12–18 inches apart, singly or in groups of 3, in sun to partial shade. Because of the weight of the flower heads, plants should be supported with stakes and string or round wire supports. Division is seldom necessary except when increase is desired. Propagate by seeds, divisions, cuttings, or leaves.

Checkerbloom *(Sidalcea malviflora)*

Also sold as *S. × hybrida* and sometimes called Prairie Mallow, Checkerbloom is a result of hybridizing several western American native species. Resembling a miniature hollyhock, Checkerbloom forms a narrow, upright plant that is excellent for the middle to back of the flower border. Growing 18–40 inches tall, the plants have fingerlike lobed leaves. The 1½-inch flowers may be pink, rose, or purple; they are borne on many-flowered spires. Plants bloom in midsummer; if flower stalks are removed after blooming, there will be flowers again in the fall. Plants are available in mixed colors or as named cultivars. Shown here is 'Loveliness', 1½–3¼ feet tall.

GROWING TIPS

Checkerbloom is easily grown in average, moist, well-drained soil. Plant in small groups, spacing plants 12–16 inches apart, in full sun. Cut back faded flowering stems for rebloom. Divide clumps after the fourth year in spring or fall. Plants may be started from seeds.

Goldenrod (*Solidago*)

Unfairly blamed for hay fever (the actual culprit is ragweed), goldenrod would be a prized garden flower if it were not so abundant in the wild. Hybridization in Europe has produced some exceptional cultivars with large flower heads and compact growth. Growing 1–5 feet high, goldenrods have small, narrow, toothed leaves. The dense, pointed clusters of flowers may be yellow to bright gold. Cultivars include 'Cloth of Gold', growing 18 inches tall with primrose-yellow flowers starting in midsummer; and 'Crown of Rays', 2 feet high with summer-blooming, flaring plumes. The compact 'Gold Dwarf', 12 inches high with yellow flowers, is seen here.

GROWING TIPS

Goldenrods are very easy to grow in moist, well-drained soil. In very rich soil, they may develop more foliage than flowers. Plant in groups of 3, spacing plants 12 inches apart, in sun to partial shade. Plants are basically pest-free and do not require staking. Divide after 4 years. Some species may self-sow.

Big Betony *(Stachys macrantha)*

Sometimes listed in catalogues as *S. grandiflora,* Big Betony grows 12–18 inches high with heart-shaped, thick, wrinkled, hairy leaves. The mintlike flowers are 1½ inches long, in 20- to 30-flowered whorls on spikes that extend above the foliage. Big Betony flowers in midsummer; the spikes are excellent for cutting. Another betony for the garden looks totally different; Lamb's-Ears, or Woolly Betony *(S. byzantina),* has large leaves covered with soft, white, woolly hairs. These form mats 4–6 inches high and up to 24 inches wide. Spikes of 1-inch purple flowers extend 12 inches above the leaves in summer. Lamb's-Ears is used as an edging and for the front of the flower border. It may be listed as *S. lanata* or *S. olympica,* and is hardy to zone 5.

GROWING TIPS

Betony is easy to grow in average, well-drained soil in full sun; Big Betony also tolerates partial shade. Space plants 12 inches apart. Division in the early spring or fall may be necessary after about 4 years. Also propagated from seeds.

Carolina Thermopsis *(Thermopsis caroliniana)* Zone 3

Carolina Thermopsis grows 3–5 feet tall with stout stems and 3-parted leaves. Blooming from late spring to early summer, the pealike flowers, ½–¾ inch across, grow in dense spikes 8–10 inches tall. Native to North America, Carolina Thermopsis is very hardy and has no pests. Established plants may form clumps up to 36 inches wide. Plants may also be sold as *T. villosa.*

GROWING TIPS

Carolina Thermopsis does best in well-drained soil in full sun, but it will tolerate even relatively infertile soil. It is quite drought resistant and withstands neglect. Plants may require staking. Propagate by division in spring or sow fresh seeds; seeds may be slow to germinate.

Hungarian Speedwell (*Veronica latifolium*)

One of the most desired of a large group of garden plants, Hungarian Speedwell grows 12–18 inches tall; it has ½-inch flowers on loose spikes that bloom for many weeks from late spring to midsummer. The cultivar 'Crater Lake Blue', seen here, is more compact. Japanese Speedwell (*V. grandis* var. *holophylla,* to zone 5) grows 2–3 feet high, with small blue flowers on 6-inch spikes; 'Lavender Charm' has lavender-blue flowers. Spike Speedwell (*V. spicata,* to zone 4) grows 12–18 inches high with ¼-inch blue flowers on 6-inch stems; there are many cultivars in pink, blue, purple, and white. The flowers of all varieties are good for cutting. By carefully choosing from among the various cultivars, you can be sure of colorful blooms from early spring to late summer.

GROWING TIPS

Speedwells are easy to grow in average, well-drained garden soil. Plant singly or in groups of 3, spacing 12 inches apart, in sun to partial shade. Divide clumps about every 4 years after flowering.

Soapweed (*Yucca glauca*)

Forming a spiky mound of pointed, narrow, white-edged leaves nearly 3 feet tall, Soapweed is a dramatic plant for use as an accent in the flower border or landscape. In summer, Soapweed sends up spikes 4–5 feet tall, covered with 2-inch-wide, greenish-white flowers. Adam's Needle (*Y. filamentosa*) is more commonly cultivated in the East. The flower stalk may be 3–15 feet high, although it usually grows to 4–5 feet. Flowers may be pure white or cream-colored. There is also a form with variegated leaves. The waxy, nodding flowers of both species are usually fragrant at night.

GROWING TIPS

Yuccas grow best in well-drained, sandy loam. Poor soil is tolerated, and plants are almost indestructible once established. Space plants 3 feet apart in full sun. Division of offsets is difficult and is best attempted in spring. Plants may also be propagated from seeds.

APPENDICES

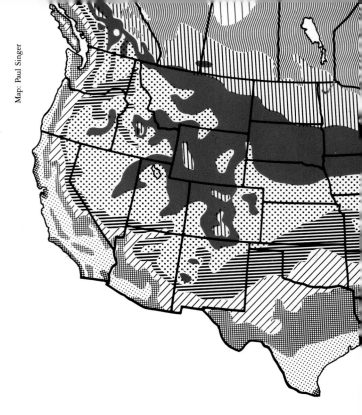

Map: Paul Singer

HARDINESS ZONE MAP

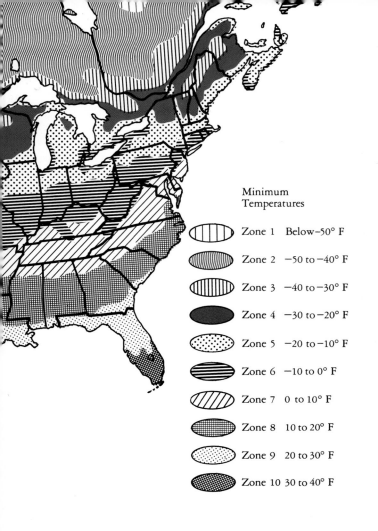

Minimum
Temperatures

Zone 1   Below −50° F

Zone 2   −50 to −40° F

Zone 3   −40 to −30° F

Zone 4   −30 to −20° F

Zone 5   −20 to −10° F

Zone 6   −10 to 0° F

Zone 7   0 to 10° F

Zone 8   10 to 20° F

Zone 9   20 to 30° F

Zone 10 30 to 40° F

GARDEN PESTS AND DISEASES

PLANT PESTS and diseases are a fact of life for a gardener. Therefore, it is helpful to become familiar with common pests and diseases in your area and to learn how to control them.

Symptoms of Plant Problems

Because the same general symptoms are associated with many diseases and pests, some experience is needed to determine their causes.

Diseases

Both fungi and bacteria are responsible for a variety of diseases ranging from leaf spots and wilts to root rot, but bacterial diseases usually make the affected plant tissues appear wetter than fungi do. Diseases caused by viruses and mycoplasma, often transmitted by aphids and leafhoppers, display such symptoms as mottled yellow or deformed leaves and twisted or stunted growth.

Insect Pests

Numerous insects attack plants. Sap-sucking insects—including aphids, leafhoppers, and scale insects—suck plant juices. The affected plant becomes yellow, stunted, and misshapen.

Aphids and scale insects produce honeydew, a sticky substance that attracts ants and sooty mold fungus growth. Other pests with rasping-sucking mouthparts, such as thrips and spider mites, scrape plant tissue and then suck the juices that well up in the injured areas.

Leaf-chewers, namely beetles and caterpillars, consume plant leaves, whole or in part. Leaf miners make tunnels within the leaves, creating brown trails and causing leaf tissue to dry. In contrast, borers tunnel into shoots and stems, and their young larvae consume plant tissue, weakening the plant. Some insects, such as various grubs and maggots, feed on roots, weakening or killing the plant.

Nematodes

Microscopic roundworms called nematodes are other pests that attack roots and cause stunting and poor plant growth. Some kinds of nematodes produce galls on roots, while others produce them on leaves.

Environmental Stresses

Some types of plant illness result from environment-related stress, such as severe wind, drought, flooding, or extreme cold. Other problems are caused by salt toxicity, rodents, birds, nutritional deficiencies or excesses, pesticides, or damage from lawn mowers. Many of these injuries are avoidable if you take proper precautions.

Controlling Plant Problems

Always buy healthy disease- and insect-free plants, and select resistant varieties when available. Check leaves and stems for dead areas or off-color and stunted tissue. Later, when you plant your flowers, be sure to prepare the soil properly.

Routine Preventives

By cultivating the soil routinely you will expose insects and disease-causing organisms to the sun and thus lessen their chances of surviving in your garden. In the fall be sure to destroy infested or diseased plants, remove dead leaves and flowers, and clean up plant debris. Do not add diseased or infested material to the compost pile. Spray plants with water from time to time to dislodge insect pests and remove suffocating dust. Pick off the larger insects by hand. To discourage fungal leaf spots and blights, always water plants in the morning and allow the leaves to dry off before nightfall. For the same reason, provide adequate air circulation around leaves and stems by spacing plants properly.

Weeds provide a home for insects and diseases, so pull them up or use herbicides. But do not apply herbicides, including "weed-and-feed" lawn preparations, too close to flower beds. Herbicide injury may cause leaves to become elongated, straplike, or downward-cupping. Spray weed-killers when there is little air movement, but not on a very hot, dry day.

Insecticides and Fungicides

To protect plant tissue from injury due to insects and diseases, a number of insecticides and fungicides are available. However, few products control diseases due to bacteria, viruses, and mycoplasma. Pesticides are usually either "protectant" or "systemic" in nature. Protectants keep insects or disease organisms away from uninfected foliage, while systemics move through the plant and provide some therapeutic or eradicant action as well as protection. Botanical insecticides such as pyrethrum and rotenone have a shorter residual effect on pests, but are considered less toxic and generally safer for the user and the environment than inorganic chemical insecticides. Biological control through the use of organisms like *Bacillus thuringiensis* (a bacterium toxic to moth and butterfly larvae) is effective and safe.

Recommended pesticides may vary to some extent from region to region. Consult your local Cooperative Extension Service or plant professional regarding the appropriate material to use. Always check the pesticide label to be sure that it is registered for use on the pest and plant with which you are dealing. Follow the label concerning safety precautions, dosage, and frequency of application.

GLOSSARY

Acid soil
Soil with a pH value of 6 or lower.

Alkaline soil
Soil with a pH value of more than 7.

Annual
A plant whose entire life span, from sprouting to flowering and producing seeds, is encompassed in a single growing season. Annuals survive cold or dry seasons as dormant seeds. See also Biennial and Perennial.

Axil
The angle formed by a leafstalk and the stem from which it grows.

Basal leaf
A leaf at the base of stem.

Beard
A fringelike growth on a petal, as in many irises.

Biennial
A plant whose life span extends to two growing seasons, sprouting in the first growing season and then flowering, producing seed, and dying in the second. See also Annual and Perennial.

Bract
A modified and often scalelike leaf, usually located at the base of a flower, a fruit, or a cluster of flowers or fruits.

Bud
A young and undeveloped leaf, flower, or shoot, usually covered tightly with scales.

Bulb
A short underground stem, the swollen portion consisting mostly of fleshy, food-storing scale leaves.

Calyx
Collectively, the sepals of a flower.

Compound leaf
A leaf made up of two or more leaflets.

Corm
A solid underground stem, resembling a bulb but lacking scales; often with a membranous coat.

Corolla
Collectively, the petals of a flower.

Corona
A crownlike structure on some corollas, as in daffodils.

Cross-pollination
The transfer of pollen from one plant to another.

Crown
That part of a plant between the roots and the stem, usually at soil level.

Cultivar
An unvarying plant variety, maintained by vegetative propagation or by inbred seed.

Cutting
A piece of plant without roots; set in a rooting medium, it develops roots, and is then potted as a new plant.

Dead-heading
Removing blooms that are spent.

Deciduous
Dropping its leaves; not evergreen.

Disbudding
The pinching off of selected buds to benefit those left to grow.

Division
Propagation by division of crowns or tubers into segments that can be induced to send out roots.

Double-flowered
Having more than the usual number of petals, usually arranged in extra rows.

Drooping
Pendant or hanging, as in the branches and shoots of a weeping willow.

Evergreen
Retaining leaves for most or all of an annual cycle.

Fertile
Bearing both stamens and pistils, and therefore able to produce seed.

Floret
One of many very small flowers in a dense flower cluster, especially in the flower heads of the daisy family.

Genus
A group of closely related species; plural, genera.

Herb
A plant without a permanent, woody stem, usually dying back during cold weather.

Herbaceous perennial
An herb that dies back each fall, but sends out new shoots and flowers for several successive years.

Horticulture
The cultivation of plants for ornament or food.

Humus
Partly or wholly decomposed vegetable matter; an important constituent of garden soil.

Hybrid
A plant resulting from a cross between two parent plants belonging to different species, subspecies, or genera.

Invasive
Aggressively spreading away from cultivation.

Lateral bud
A bud borne in the axil of a leaf or branch; not terminal.

Layering
A method of propagation in which a stem is induced to send out roots by surrounding it with soil.

Leaf axil
The angle between the petiole of a leaf and the stem to which it is attached.

Leaflet
One of the subdivisions of a compound leaf.

Loam
A humus-rich soil containing up to 25 percent clay, up to 50 percent silt, and less than 50 percent sand.

Lobe
A segment of a cleft leaf or petal.

Midrib
The primary rib or mid-vein of a leaf or leaflet.

Mulch
A protective covering spread over the soil around the base of plants to retard evaporation, control temperature, or enrich the soil.

Naturalized
Established as a part of the flora in an area other than the place of origin.

Neutral soil
Soil that is neither acid nor alkaline, having a pH value of 7.

Node
The place on the stem where leaves or branches are attached.

Offset
A short, lateral shoot arising near the base of a plant, readily producing new roots, and useful in propagation.

Perennial
A plant whose life span extends over several growing seasons and that produces seeds in several growing seasons, rather than only one. See also Annual and Biennial.

Petal
One of a series of flower parts lying within the sepals and next to the stamens and pistils, often large and brightly colored.

Petiole
The stalk of a leaf.

pH
A symbol for the hydrogen ion content of the soil, and thus a means of expressing the acidity or alkalinity of the soil.

Pistil
The female reproductive organ of a flower, consisting of an ovary, style, and stigma.

Pollen
Minute grains containing the male germ cells and released by the stamens.

Propagate
To produce new plants, either by vegetative means involving the rooting of pieces of a plant, or by sowing seeds.

Prostrate
Lying on the ground; creeping.

Raceme
A long flower cluster on which individual flowers each bloom on small stalks from a common, larger, central stalk.

Ray flower
A flower at the edge of a flowerhead of the daisy family, usually bearing a conspicuous, straplike ray.

Rhizomatous
Having rhizomes.

Rhizome
A horizontal underground stem, distinguished from a root by the presence of nodes, and often enlarged by food storage.

Rootstock
The swollen, more or less elongate stem of a perennial herb.

Rosette
A crowded cluster of leaves; usually basal, circular, and at ground level.

Runner
A prostrate shoot, rooting at its nodes.

Sepal
One of the outermost series of flower parts, arranged in a ring outside the petals, and usually green and leaflike.

Solitary
Borne singly or alone; not in clusters.

Spathe
A bract or pair of bracts, often large, enclosing the flowers, as in members of the Arum family.

Species
A population of plants or animals whose members are at least potentially able to breed with each other, but which is reproductively isolated from other populations.

Spike
An elongated flower cluster; individual flowers lack stalks.

Stamen
The male reproductive organ of a flower, consisting of a filament and a pollen-containing anther.

Sterile
Lacking stamens or pistils, and therefore not capable of producing seeds.

Subspecies
A naturally occurring geographical variant of a species.

Taproot
The main, central root of a plant.

Terminal bud
A bud borne at the tip of a stem or shoot, rather than in the axil of a leaf. See also Lateral bud.

Terminal raceme
A raceme borne at the tip of the main stem of a plant.

Terminal spike
A spike borne at the tip of the main stem of a plant.

Throat
The opening between the bases of the corolla lobes of a flower, leading into the corolla tube.

Toothed
Having the margin shallowly divided into small, toothlike segments.

Tuber
A swollen, mostly underground stem that bears buds and serves as a storage site for food.

Tufted
Growing in dense clumps, cushions, or tufts.

Variegated.
Marked, striped, or blotched with some color other than green.

Variety
A population of plants that differ consistently from the typical form of the species, either occurring naturally or produced in cultivation.

Vegetative propagation
Propagation by means other than seed.

Whorl
A group of three or more leaves or shoots, all emerging from a stem at a single node.

Whorled
Arranged along a twig or shoot in groups of three or more at each node.

PHOTO CREDITS

INDEX

CHANTICLEER PRESS
STEWART, TABORI & CHANG

Publisher
ANDREW STEWART

Senior Editor
ANN WHITMAN

Production
KATHY ROSENBLOOM
KARYN SLUTSKY

Design
JOSEPH RUTT